A STUDY OF CANON 2222, § 1

THE CATHOLIC UNIVERSITY OF AMERICA
CANON LAW STUDIES
No. 290

A Study of Canon 2222, § 1

A HISTORICAL SYNOPSIS AND A COMMENTARY

BY

REVEREND JAMES V. CASEY, B.A., J.C.L.
PRIEST OF THE ARCHDIOCESE OF DUBUQUE

A DISSERTATION

SUBMITTED TO THE FACULTY OF THE SCHOOL OF CANON LAW OF THE CATHOLIC UNIVERSITY OF AMERICA IN PARTIAL FULFILLMENT OF THE REQUIREMENTS FOR THE DEGREE OF DOCTOR OF CANON LAW

THE CATHOLIC UNIVERSITY OF AMERICA PRESS
WASHINGTON, D. C.
1949

Nihil Obstat:

LUDOVICUS MOTRY, S.T.D., J.C.D.
Censor Deputatus
Washingtonii, die 15 iunii, 1949

Imprimatur:

✠ HENRY P. ROHLMAN, D.D.
Archiepiscopus Dubuquensis
Dubuquii, die 18 iunii, 1949

PRINTED BY
LORAS COLLEGE PRESS
DUBUQUE, IOWA

RESPECTFULLY DEDICATED WITH GRATITUDE

To

THE MOST REV. HENRY P. ROHLMAN, D.D., LL.D.
Archbishop of Dubuque

TABLE OF CONTENTS

PART TWO

CANONICAL COMMENTARY

CHAPTER VI

CHAPTER VII

CHAPTER VIII

FOREWORD

The right of the Church to enact and to impose canonical penalties is called a "ius nativum et proprium";[1] from the earliest times, the first Apostles of Christ were mindful that in their mission "to teach all nations"[2] they had been fortified with more than the power of persuasion. For Our Lord had identified His own universal power "in heaven and on earth"[3] with the authority that He had transmitted to His Church, and no limitation was placed on the power "to bind and to loose."[4]

In the early Church, before a system of penal law had developed, the use of coercive authority, of necessity, was left to the discretion of the individual bishops. A study of the development of penal power in ecclesiastical legislation reveals a policy of gradual restriction and regulation of this discretionary penal authority in the interests of justice and as a safeguard against possible tyrannical abuse.

With the Code of Canon Law, there appeared for the first time a well-defined system of penal law. The subject of this study, canon 2222, §1, takes on importance from the fact that it represents a certain essential residuum of the rather broad discretional penal authority that heretofore had existed as an integral part of ecclesiastical law. Although this canon incorporates the principle *nulla poena sine lege* as a guarantee of the rights of individuals against despotic severity, at the same time it provides a safeguard against possible abuse of this protection by those who would not hesitate to jeopardize the spiritual commonweal of the Mystical Body of Christ.

1 Canon 2214, § 1; cf. Ottaviani, *Compendium Iuris Publici Ecclesiastici* (Typis Polyglottis Vaticanis, 1936), p. 99.

2 Matth., XXVIII, 18.

3 Matth., XXVIII, 18.

4 Matth., XXVIII, 19.

The prescripts of this canon represent a skillful blend of hierarchical penal authority with democratic safeguards that protect the rights of the faithful. It is hoped that this study of the penal principles that underlie this canon will contribute in some little way to a better understanding of the mind of the law-giver as reflected in the Code of Canon Law.

The writer welcomes this occasion to acknowledge his sincere gratitude to the Most Reverend Henry P. Rohlman, Archbishop of Dubuque, for the opportunity of advanced study in Canon Law at The Catholic University of America. The writer is grateful also to the members of the Faculty of the School of Canon Law for their discerning guidance and direction during the three-year course of studies. And to the many others who gave generously of their time and encouragement during the preparation of this dissertation, the writer acknowledges his debt of gratitude.

PART I

HISTORICAL SYNOPSIS

CHAPTER ONE

STATUS OF PENAL LAW IN THE EARLY CHURCH

INTRODUCTION

The principle if not the formula *nulla poena sine lege* constitutes the fundamental substance of canon 2222, §1, which is the subject of this study. In virtue of this canon the ordinary penal norm requires that no canonical sanction be inflicted unless an admonition with the threat of a penalty has preceded;[1] thus the legislator affords a guarantee to the faithful that promises protection from possible injustice or tyranny.

In this same penal statute the legislator serves notice that the principle *nulla poena sine lege* shall be accorded a broad and liberal construction which conforms to the needs of the Church, whose *lex suprema* is the salvation of souls. This extraordinary norm provides for the use of coercive power against the violations of non-penal laws when notable scandal or special gravity jeopardizes the spiritual welfare of the religious society.[2]

The canons of the present Code in a large majority do not contain in each individual juridic obligation the specific threat of a penal sanction. The provision in cases of notable scandal or of specially grave transgressions as enacted in canon 2222, §1, constitutes an extraordinary residue of discretionary penal authority that can be employed by lawful superiors against those who otherwise could abuse the protection afforded the faithful in the ordinary penal norms.

1 "...reus puniri nequit, nisi prius monitus fuerit cum comminatione poenae latae vel ferendae sententiae in casu transgressionis, et nihilominus legem violaverit."

2 "Licet lex nullam sanctionem appositam habeat, legitimus tamen Superior potest illius transgressionem, etiam sine praevia poenae comminatione, aliqua iusta poena punire, si scandalum forte datum aut specialis transgressionis gravitas id ferat..."

ARTICLE I. THE USE OF COERCIVE POWER

After centuries of gradual development, a highly perfected system of *procedure* was in operation throughout the Church long before the Council of Trent (1545-1563).[3] However, the history of the development of penal doctrine does not manifest the same systematic advance. The fact is that penal law did not receive distinct treatment separately from procedural law until the thirteenth century when Bernard of Pavia (+1213) in the so-called *Compilatio Prima* devoted several separate titles to the consideration of delicts and penalties. Subsequent authentic collections employed the same arrangement, but it was not until the present legislation of the Code was promulgated that an articulate and systematic penal doctrine took its rightful place in a separate and distinct canonical department.[4] Heretofore that precision which had so admirably directed the other departments of canon law was not found in the penal law of the Church.[5] This lack of a universal penal system should be kept in mind in an investigation of the historical background of canon 2222, § 1.

During the first three centuries the exercise of coercive power was exclusively in the hands of the bishops. Their judicial decisions were recognized by secular rulers after the fourth century, and the penal sanctions which they imposed were sometimes enforced with the aid of the secular government.[6] Hinschius (1835-1898) pointed out that the coercive power of bishops in the ancient discipline had few restrictions, and that any grave disturbance of public order was punished by him without regard to pre-existing juric obligations or previous admonitions.[7]

[3] "Damnari non valet nisi convictus aut sponte confessus." —c. 1, C. II, q. 1.

[4] "...in futuro codice iuris ecclesiastici, sua, ut sperare licit, erit pars, in qua et principia iuris poenalis et singula delicta cum respectivis poenis ordine systematico proponantur, atque dubia et incertitudines iuris poenalis penitus tollantur."—Wernz, *Ius Decretalium* (6 vols., Romae, 1898-1905), VI, 6.

[5] The Constitution *Apostolicae Sedis* of Pius IX, issued on October 12, 1869, simply catalogued such delicts to which *latae sententiae* censures were attached.

[6] Hinschius, *Das Kirchenrecht der Katholiken und Protestanten in Deutschland* (6 vols., Berlin, 1869-1897), IV, 763 (hereafter cited *Kirchenrecht*).

[7] *Kirchenrecht*, IV, 745; V, 295 and 906.

The Council of Antioch (341) spoke of the coercive power attached to the episcopal office,[8] as did also the Council of Sardica (343).[9] In his letters, Pope Gregory the Great (590-604) made frequent reference to the penal authority of the bishops, and insisted that the exercise of this power was indigenous to the episcopal office.[10] Indications of the extensive penal power of the bishop are found in every age; in a Roman synod held in 898, Pope John IX (898-900) declared:

> Habeant igitur episcopi singularium urbium in suis dioecesibus liberam potestatem adulteria et scelera inquirere, ulcisci et iudicare, secundum quod canones censent, absque impedimento alicuius.[11]

From the pseudo-Isidorian decretals, Gratian incorporated in his *Decretum* a number of letters attributed to the early popes. The text of these decretal letters pointed to the absolute power of the bishops in penal matters during the period of the early Church. A letter ascribed to Pope St. Clement I (88-97) insisted on the absolute authority of the bishop,[12] and Pope St. Urban I (222-230) was reputed to have stated that a canonical penalty inflicted by any bishop was to be acknowledged by the world: *"Valde timenda est sententia episcopi, licet iniuste liget."*[13] These letters of spurious origin borrowed importance from the fact that as time went on they were accepted as law and found their way into the *Decree* of Gratian.

This lack of a universal and well-defined penal system necessarily left the administration of penal law to the arbitrary judgment of the bishops.[14] However, the development of a

[8] C. 12—Hardouin, *Acta Conciliorum et Epistolae Decretales ac Constitutiones Summorum Pontificum* (12 vols., Parisiis, 1714-1715), I, 598 (hereafter cited Hardouin).

[9] Cc. 7 and 11—Bruns, *Canones Apostolorum et Conciliorum Saeculorum IV-VII* (2 vols., Berolini, 1839), I, 93, 99 (hereafter cited Bruns).

[10] Mansi, *Sacrorum Conciliorum Nova et Amplissima Collectio* (53 vols., Paris-Arnhem-Leipzig, 1901-1927), X, 270 (hereafter cited Mansi); c. 23, D. LXXVI.

[11] C. 1, X, de *officio iudicis ordinarii,* I, 31.

[12] C. 11, C. XI, q. 3.

[13] C. 27, C. XI, q. 3.

[14] "...episcopi poterant quoslibet perturbationes poenis compescere adepta libertate."—Roberti, *De Delictis et Poenis* (2 vols., Romae: Pontificium Institutum Utriusque Iuris, 1930-1938), I, 6.

procedural order brought with it restrictions on the exercise of penal authority.

ARTICLE II. DEVELOPMENT OF A PENAL SYSTEM

During the fourth century the age of persecutions ended and was replaced with a period of favor from the State. Under this newly-won freedom, the conversion of the Empire's population to the faith brought with it a multiplication of crime both in kind and in number. The need of a uniform and universal penal system became more acute; this complexity of disciplinary problems called forth a series of instructions and regulations with a view to the salutary administration of coercive power.[15] It is noted however that this development in penal law took place incidental to and within the framework of *judicial procedure.*

In the writings of St. Augustine (354-430) which were later to form a part of Gratian's *Decretum* there was a constant insistence on the need of judicial procedure before a penal sentence could be pronounced;[16] the need for an equitable proportion between the crime and the penalty was stressed,[17] and it was maintained that uncertain and dubious delicts were not to be punished.[18]

There is some evidence that the bishop was expected to take counsel with his priests before he inflicted a penalty although it does not seem that this requirement pertained to validity. St. Cyprian (+258) indicated this,[19] and the IV Council of Carthage (398) reaffirmed the need of the presence of the clergy when the bishop pronounced his sentence upon the hearing of a case.[20] The letters of Pope Gregory the Great

15 Bourret, *Des Sentences Ecclésiastiques* (Montpellier, 1909), p. 19.

16 "Nos a communione prohibere quemquam non possumus... nisi aut sponte confessum, aut in aliquo sive saeculari sive ecclesiastico iudicio nominatum atque convictum."—c. 18, C. II, q. 1; Migne, *Patrologiae Cursus Completus, Series Latina* (221 vols., Parisiis, 1844-1855), XXXIX, 1546 (hereafter cited *MPL*); cf. also c. 1, 15, 17, 18, C. II, q. 1.

17 C. 21, C. XXIV, q. 1; c. 19, C. XXII, q. 4.

18 C. I, C. II, q. 1.

19 *S. Thasci Caecilii Cypriani Omnia Opera, Ep. XVI—Corpus Scriptorum Ecclesiasticorum Latinorum* (68 vols., Vindobonae, 1866-), III, pars 2, p. 527 (hereafter cited *CSEL*); *MPL*, IV, 261.

20 Can. 23—"Ut Episcopus nullius causam audiat absque praesentia clericorum suorum, alioquin irrita erit sententia episcopi, nisi clericorum praesentia confirmetur."—Bruns, I, 144.

spoke of penalties inflicted "*presentibus ecclesiae tuae senioribus,*"[21] and in a letter to the Bishop of Corinth, Pope Gregory warned against the arbitrary and hasty imposition of penalties.[22] Early in the sixth century the Council of Agde (506) issued legislation to restrain the arbitrary infliction of penalties, and established sanctions against those prelates who ignored the prescripts of this Council.[23]

The Council of Agde also introduced the requirement that three previous admonitions were to be issued before the penalty of suspension or excommunication could be inflicted.[24] Pope Gregory the Great in 592 referred to these previous warnings as required "*ex necessitate.*"[25] This same requirement was promulgated at the Council of Mainz (851).[26]

The failure to observe this requirement was condemned at the III General Council of the Lateran (1179) as a "*reprehensibilis valde consuetudo.*" The Council stated:

> We declare in the present decree that prelates shall not without previous canonical warning impose on their subjects the sentence of suspension or excommunication, unless the offense be such that by nature it calls for the penalty of excommunication without warning.[27]

In 1215 the IV General Council of the Lateran reaffirmed this necessity,[28] as did also Pope Innocent IV (1243-1254) at

[21] C. 23, D. LXXXVI; Jaffé, *Regesta Pontificum Romanorum ab condita ecclesia ad annum post Christum natum MCXCVIII,* (2. ed., G. Wattenbach, F. Kaltenbrunner, P. Ewald, S. Loewenfeld, 2 vols., Lipsiae, 1885-1888) n. 1911 (hereafter cited Jaffé).

[22] *Loc. cit.*

[23] Can. 3—Bruns, II, 146; Hardouin, II, 998; c. 8, C. XI, q. 3.

[24] Can. 3—Mansi, VIII, 338.

[25] *Ep. 52* (ad Natalem)—*MPL,* LXXVII, 598; Jaffé n. 1204.

[26] Can. 8—*Monumenta Germaniae Historica, Leges* (5 vols., Vols. I-IV ed. G. Pertz; Vol. V, edd. G. Pertz, G. Waitz, H. Brunner, Hannover, 1835-1889), I, 413 (hereafter cited *MGH*).

[27] Can. 6—Schroeder, *Disciplinary Decrees of the General Councils; Text, Translation, and Commentary* (St. Louis: Herder, 1937), p. 220; Hardouin, VII, 1676; c. 26, X, *de appellationibus, recusationibus et relationibus,* II, 28.

[28] Can. 47—c. 48, X, *de sententia excommunicationis,* V, 39; Mansi, XXII, 1031.

the I General Council of Lyons (1245)[29] and Pope Gregory X (1271-1276) at the II General Council of Lyons (1274).[30] Pope Boniface VIII (1294-1303) declared the sentences of excommunication invalid unless they were issued in conformity with these regulations.[31]

It is important to note that in every case these conciliar decrees were later incorporated in the *Corpus Iuris Canonici.* In regard to this legislation which required the issuance of admonitions, their necessity was restricted to the infliction of suspension and excommunication; in conformity with the concept of the present legislation in canon 2222, §1, it is also to be noted that the Councils took cognizance of the fact that under certain extraordinary conditions it was lawful to omit these specific warnings.[32]

It was manifest however that the general historical trend was one that sought to regulate and restrict the exercise of penal authority. The mind of the Church appeared set against harshness, and its penal prescripts seemed to grant the delinquent some favor of the law rather than to jeopardize the rights of the faithful through any possible perpetration of injustice. In this trend one may discern the early traces of the basic concepts inherent in the legal axiom *nulla poena sine lege.*

ARTICLE III. PROVISION IN CASES OF SERIOUS SCANDAL AND OF SPECIALLY GRAVE TRANSGRESSIONS

In spite of this trend to a strict adherence to canonical procedure, the sources reveal a constant vigilance on the part of the Church to provide legal remedies for counteracting the evil effects of serious scandal and of extraordinarily perverse crimes. The special faculty enacted in canon 2222, §1, conforms to this canonical tradition. Canonical history in the

29 C. 3, *de sententia excommunicationis, suspensionis et interdicti* V, 11, in VI°; Mansi, XXIII, 622; cf. Schroeder, *op. cit.*, p. 306.

30 Can. 24—Mansi, XXIV, 101; c. 2, *de censibus, exactionibus et procurationibus,* III, 20, in VI°.

31 "...praecipimus inviolabiliter observari, decernentes easdem sententias non tenere aliter promulgatas."—c. 13, *de sententia excommunicationis, suspensionis, et interdicti,* V. 11, in VI°.

32 Can. 24—II General Council of Lyons, Mansi, XXIV, 101; c. 2, *de censibus, exactionibus et procurationibus,* III, 20, in VI°.

sources reveals that such provision was seen as an *extraordinary* derogation, postulated as necessary in the very concept of the Church's supernatural mission. In this regard it is important to recall that the penal doctrine of the Church developed as a matter closely related to procedure, and until a late date it was not treated separately from procedure. Consequently in many cases it was the canonical procedure that reflected the historical tradition for the extraordinary remedy that could be invoked in cases of notable scandal and of specially grave transgressions.

The legislation current during the middle ages required a strict adherence to the *ordo iudiciarius* if a canonical penalty was to be inflicted upon a deliquent. This was the universal practice by the time of Gratian: *"Quod autem nullus sine iudiciario ordine damnari valeat, multis auctoritatibus probatur.*[33] However, the legislation provided that whenever the crime was notorious and evident[34] the judicial order, which called for a formal accusation, admonitions, the testimony of witnesses and the gathering of evidence, could be dispensed with and a proportionate penalty inflicted immediately.[35] In many cases the element of notoriety aggravated the enormity of the crime and of the scandal so that the immediate application of punitive measures was necessitated beyond all question.

Papal instructions and conciliar decrees recognized the need of an extraordinary penal remedy under these conditions, and they frequently directed the bishops to act with dispatch when the seriousness of the scandal or the enormity of the crime required it. The Council of Agde (506) instructed ecclesiastical superiors to suspend immediately any member of the clergy who was the source of constant scandal, even when judicial proof was lacking, "*. . .ne populus fidelium in eo scandalum patiatur.*"[36] The commentators on this decree added that this

[33] *Dictum Gratiani* ad c. 1, C. II, q. 1.

[34] "Manifestum est quod semper ex scientia et ex certo auctore procedit, et quod potest probari. . ."—*Glossa Ordinaria,* s.v. *manifesta,* ad c. 15, C. II, q. 1.

[35] "Docet Gratianus quod crimen dicatur manifestum quod negari non potest: cum se ingerat oculis omnium: in quo ordo iudiciarius non requiritur. . ."—*Glossa Ordinaria* ad *Dictum Gratiani,* c. 17, C. II, q. 1; c. 8, X, *de cohabitatione clericorum et mulierum,* III, 2.

[36] Mansi, VIII, 338; *MGH, Leges,* I, 413; c. 2, X, *de purgatione canonica,* V, 34.

derogation from the usual canonical procedure was never justified unless the special seriousness of the delict or the imminence of scandal demanded the immediate infliction of suspension without previous warning.[37] In this regard there arose among the commentators the question whether this manner of procedure in the inflicting of a suspension could be utilized also for the deprivation of an ecclesiastical benefice. They answered that ordinarily the *ordo iudicarius* had to be followed if a cleric was to be deprived of his benefice.[38] But Panormitanus (1386-1453) pointed out that the immediate suspension of a priest both from his office and from his benefice was permissible if it was warranted by the enormity of the scandal or of the crime.[39]

The II General Council of Lyons (1274) issued legislation concerning the needed intervals of several days between the three warnings that preceded the infliction of the penalty of excommunication.[40] However, the severity of this requirement was tempered through the special provision that allowed the omission of the warnings when *"facti necessitas aliter ea suaserit moderanda."*[41] In commenting on this provision Ioannes Andreae (1272-1348) taught that the omission of the admonitions was warranted whenever there was question of a crime committed under such circumstances that immediate punitive action was necessary and warnings could not prove of any avail.[42]

A letter of Pope Innocent III (1198-1216), in 1199, illustrates the application of this special derogation from the usual norm of procedure when the danger of great scandal or the extraordinary seriousness of the crime required it.[43] The

37 "Numquam a principio suspendat eum nisi enormitas delict vel scandali hoc exposcat."—*Glossa Ordinaria*, s.v. *suspendatur*, ad c. 13, C. II, q. 5.

38 *Glossa Ordinaria*, ad c. 13, C. II, q. 5, s.v. *suspendatur*.

39 "Infamatus non debet regulariter suspendi a beneficio antequam deficiat in purgatione, sed ratione enormitatis criminis, vel scandali imminentis, potest suspendi etiam a beneficio donec se purgaverit."—*Omnia Quae Extant Commentaria in Decretales* (6 vols., Venetiis, 1588), ad. c. 10, X, *de purgatione canonica*, V, 34 (hereafter cited *Commentaria*).

40 Cf. C. 9, X, *de sententia excommunicationes*, V, 11.

41 *Loc. cit.*

42 *Glossa Ordinaria*, s.v. *necessitas*, ad c. 9, X, *de sententia excommunicationis*, V, 11.

43 C. 10, X, *de purgatione canonica*, V, 34.

Archbishop of the Diocese of Sens had suspended a priest from both his office and his benefice, for abundant evidence indicated that the priest had fallen into the proximate danger of heresy in the eyes of the people. The delinquent was not given a warning, and he was denied all opportunity of a canonical purgation. The Archbishop justified his mode of action *"propter immanitatem criminis"*.[44] In his reply, Pope Innocent III took cognizance of each step which had been omitted in the judicial order. He stated:

> Quia tamen eum etiam a beneficio propter immanitatem criminis suspendisti, nolumus improbare... in eo et per eum non modicum fuisse scandalum catholicorum animis declaratum. Unde propter vehementem infamiam et grave scandalum ipsum ab officio et beneficio suspendisti.[45]

Relative to this practice the commentators explained in the marginal gloss:

> Tantum propter enormitatem delicti et scandalum, et infamiam magnam inde ortam, statim potest episcopus ipsum suspendere ab officio et beneficio... et sic Huguccio (+1210) intelligit illud.[46]

Hostiensis (+1271) substantiated this doctrine that made special provision in cases of notable scandal and specially grave transgressions, and in affirmation he cited the celebrated case of King Lothaire of Lorraine (855-869).[47] It involved a divorce and remarriage by the King who was aided and abetted by an assembly of bishops in council at Aachen in the year 860. The vigorous Pontiff St. Nicholas I (858-867) dispatched two papal legates to Metz with instructions to convoke a national council and to reopen the question. However the papal legates were prevailed upon to join in common cause with the delinquents. When these decisions as formulated at Metz were published, the Pontiff declared them null and void, and dispensing with canonical procedure he levied penalties of de-

[44] C. 10, X, *de purgatione canonica,* V, 34.
[45] C. 10, X, *de purgatione canonica,* V, 34.
[46] *Glossa Ordinaria,* ad c. 10, X, *de purgatione canonica,* V, 34.
[47] *Summa Aurea* (Venetiis, 1570), p. 385.

position from office and suspension from sacred Orders against two of the guilty prelates, and ordered King Lothaire to the monastery at Monte Cassino in order that reparation for the serious scandal might be made.[48] Again this mode of action was justified by the extraordinary gravity of the scandal and of the crime.

Panormitanus took note of this special derogation when he taught that "*. . .ubi enormitas delicti, vel scandali non subest, non debet ante purgationem praestitam suspensionem facere.*"[49] The presence of this condition of notable scandal or special gravity in the crime was considered as a *sine qua non* that alone justified any radical departure from the ordinary norm whereby canonical sanctions were executed through the inflicting of penalties.

The extraordinary character of this provision in cases of serious scandal and especially grave delicts is accentuated through the fact of the stormy reception later accorded to the Tridentine legislation which became known as *suspensio ex informata conscientia.*[50]

The historical relationship between this extraordinary penal remedy and the special faculty provided in canon 2222, § 1, will be considered in the third chapter of this study. At this point it will suffice simply to note that this special penal remedy demonstrated the willingness of the Fathers of the Council to sacrifice canonical procedure only when serious scandal or the extraordinary gravity of the transgression threatened to jeopardize the spiritual good of society.

The constant tradition of ecclesiastical jurisprudence required a strict adherence to the *ordo iudiciarius* in the infliction of canonical penalties. The singular provision for cases of

[48] *Glossa Ordinaria,* s.v. *referebat,* ad c. 21, C. II, q. 1; Mansi, XV, 649. Cf. also c. 1, X, *de maledicis,* V, 26.

[49] "...ubi subesset scandalum, vel grave delictum, potest a principio suspendere ab officio...et etiam a beneficio."—*Commentaria,* ad c. 3, X, *de crimine falsi,* V, 20.

[50] *Conc. Trident.,* sess. XIV, *de ref.,* c. 1; cf. also S. C. de Prop. Fide, instr. 20 oct. 1884, n. 2—*Collectanea S. Congregationis de Propaganda Fide* (2 vols., Romae: Typographia Polyglotta S. C. de Propaganda Fide, 1907), n. 1628; *Codicis Iuris Canonici Fontes,* cura et studio Emi Petri Card. Gasparri editi (9 vols., Romae postea Civitate Vaticano: Typis Polyglottis Vaticanis, 1923-1939). (Vols. VII-IX, ed. cura et studio Emi Iustiniani Card. Seredi), n. 4907. These two collections will in future references be cited as *Collectanea* and *Fontes.*

notable scandal and specially grave transgressions, as it is now found in the legislation of canon 2222, § 1, was of exceptional application. But the penal doctrine as reflected in this canon was discernible among the commentators of the pre-Code era. In general concept their doctrine foreshadowed the later teaching of Smith (1845-1895) when he stated:

> Where the offense committed is of great enormity and therefore shows that the delinquent acted with exceeding great malice prepense, and is so to say, hardened in crime, or where the greatness of the scandal given requires it, the vindicative punishment may be inflicted at once, that is, without the previous admonitions or precepts, though not without trial.[51]

For the most part the development of a penal system in the sources demonstrated a cautious and restrained policy in the use of coercive authority.[52] At the same time the legislator in the Church has ever been mindful that Our Lord reserved His harshest condemnation for those "by whom the scandal cometh,"[53] and accordingly canonical legislation provided legal remedies with which lawful superiors could remove the danger that derived from that source whenever it threatened the spiritual well-being of those who were committed to their care.

[51] *Elements of Ecclesiastical Law* (3 vols., Vol. III, *Ecclesiastical Punishments,* Benziger Bros., New York: 1888), III, 43; cf. also Reiffenstuel, *Ius Canonicum Universum* (7 vols., Parisiis: 1864-1870), lib. V, tit. XXXIX, nn. 24, 27, 28.

[52] "...ex ipsa rerum humanarum natura repugnat, ut potestas quaedam publica omnia hominum peccata etiam externa puniat in foro externo, nisi summa introducatur confusio in societate humana.—Cui legi naturali vel ipsum exercitium potestatis ecclesiasticae est subjectum."—Suarez, *Opera Omnia* (28 vols., Vol. V, Parisiis, 1856), V, *Tractatus de Legibus et Legislatore Deo,* Lib. IV, c. 12, nn. 11, 12.

[53] Matth. XVIII, 6-8.

CHAPTER TWO

CANONICAL PRECEDENTS OF THE PRINCIPLE *NULLA POENA SINE LEGE*

ARTICLE I. DIVERSE CONCEPTS IN THE PRINCIPLE

The historical genesis of this legal axiom has been the center of controversy for a long time among both canonical and secular jurists. It represents a complex problem, and it is not within the scope of this study to analyze all the factors involved, much less to presume to offer a definitive answer to all historical problems that underlie this principle of penal science.

Nonetheless canon 2222, § 1, constitutes a canonical paraphrase of the formula *nulla poena sine lege;* it has been popular to allege the complete dependency of the Church on secular sources for the acquisition of the principle which, they say, made its debut as a product of the French Revolution in the "Declaration of the Rights of Men" on the 26th of August, 1789.[1]

The actual formula itself was coined by a German jurist, P. A. Feuerbach (1775-1833), early in the last century.[2] Certainly the temper of the times hastened the canonical adoption of the penal concepts inherent in this axiom. The political revolutions brought victory to the republican form of government; with it arose a development of penal science which found expression in explicit guarantees against discretionary penal authority. It was in this period that the penal law of the Church made great advances. Since the eighteenth century, the principle *nulla poena sine lege* has been adopted in nearly all

[1] Art. 8—"...Nul ne peut être puni qu'en vertu d'une loi établie et promulguée antérieurement au délit et légalement appliquée."

[2] *Lehrbuch des gemeinen in Deutschland geltenden peinlichen Privatrechts* (14 ed. prepared by C. J. A. Mittermaier, Giessen: G. F. Heyer, 1847), nn. 19-20.

modern secular penal codes[3] and it is evident that the development of canonical jurisprudence in this atmosphere was influenced to a great extent by the advance of penal science in secular law.

It is necessary however to understand that the legal formula *nulla poena sine lege* contains not just one but three distinct and closely inter-related legal concepts. These diverse concepts developed slowly in different periods of history. But investigation reveals that the legislator of the Code had only to turn to the sources of ecclesiastical jurisprudence for the basic but as yet unrefined concepts of this principle.[4]

The three diverse concepts contained in the axiom will be considered separately in the following order: 1) the necessity of a pre-existing penal statute; 2) the non-retroactivity of penal law; 3) the prohibition of analogy in penal law.

ARTICLE II. THE NECESSITY OF A PRIOR PENAL STATUTE

From the standpoint of the natural law, it is not necessary that a *pre-existing* penal statute be violated before the infliction of a proportionate penalty is warranted; it is sufficient to establish only that an external evil action is imputed to the delinquent.[5]

Although the Church from the earliest times distinguished between sin and crime,[6] it reserved the right to inflict punishment for evil actions whenever punitive action seemed necessary for the common good. Pope Innocent III (1198-1216) vindicated this right when he declared that every serious

[3] U.S.A., art. 1, sec. 9, n. 3; Italy, 1889, art, 1-2; Spain, 1870, art. 22; Belgium, 1867, art. 2; Norway, 1902, art. 3; one notable exception to this trend: Art. 16, *Soviet Penal Code,* 1926; cf. also *American Law and Procedure,* III (La Salle Extension University, 1943), p. 15.

[4] Giacchi, "Precedenti Canonistici del Principio 'Nullum crimen sine praevia lege poenali'," *Studi in onore di Francesco Scaduto* (2 vols., Firenze: Polygrafica Universitaria, 1936), I, 438.

[5] "Ratio est quia quoad omnes actus malos adest fundamentum iuridicum potestatis coactivae."—Michiels, *Normae Generales Iuris Canonici* (2 vols., Lublin-Polonia, Universitas Catholica, 1929), I, 201.

[6] C. 1, D. LXXXI; Wernz, *Ius Decretalium,* VI, 15.

sin can have the character of a delict;[7] and Pope Alexander III had instructed bishops to inflict some just penalty when the law made no specific provision.[8]

Until the appearance of the present Code of Canon Law, canonical writers held divergent opinions concerning the constitutive elements of an ecclesiastical delict; yet a precise and authoritative determination of these elements seems essential to this concept of the axiom *nulla poena sine lege.* In a later article the pre-Code provision for the use of discretionary or extraordinary penalties will be discussed. At this point it is simply to be noted that such a provision supports the view that before the advent of the Code the prior existence of a penal law was not an absolute and unvarying postulate for the infliction of a canonical penalty.

This is not to say that there were no traces of the concept in the early sources; in fact, the normal or ordinary practice conformed to this principle. In the opening decade of the present century, Wernz (1842-1914) argued that there could be no true ecclesiastical delict apart from the violation of a *penal statute* of the Church's law.[9] Nonetheless evidence taken from canonical sources does not support a strict adherence to this concept of the principle until modern times.[10]

ARTICLE III. THE NON-RETROACTIVITY OF PENAL LAW

The second legal concept implied in the principle *nulla poena sine lege* concerns the non-retroactivity of penal law, a concept

[7] C. 13, X, *de iudiciis,* II, 1: "... Intendimus decernere de peccato, cuius ad nos pertinet sine dubitatione censura, quam in quemlibet exercere possumus et debemus... nullus, qui sit sanae mentis, ignorat, quin ad officium nostrum spectet de quocumque mortali peccato corripere quemlibet Christianum, et, si correctionem contempserit, ipsum per districtionem ecclesiasticam coercere..."

[8] C. 4, *de officio et potestate iudicis delegati,* I, 29.

[9] "Simplex violatio legis aut praecepti sanctionem poenalem saltem indeterminatam non continentis, licet peccatum sit in foro interno Ecclesiae subjectum ac per poenitentias castigandum etiam publicas a praxi tamen vigenti non alienas, si publice et cum scandalo commissum fuerit...verum autem delictum non constituit, unde vera poena ecclesiastica a Praelato R. Pontifice inferiore puniri non potest, nisi praevia monitione comminationem poenalem continente, qua transgressori intimetur, ut a violatione desistat, vel actum lege requisitum ponat, vel scandalum forte datum reparet."—*Ius Decretalium,* VI, n. 14.

[10] Hinschius, *Kirchenrecht,* IV, 745; Lega, *De Delictis et Poenis* (2. ed., Romae, 1910), pp. 23-24.

enunciated by St. Ambrose (333-397) in the late fourth century: "*. . . poena criminis ex tempore legis est, quae crimen inhibuit, nec ante legem ulla rei damnatio est, sed ex lege.*"[11] Gratian adopted this doctrine of St. Ambrose into his *Decretum,* where the glossators elaborated upon this concept and applied it to the non-retroactivity of penal statutes.[12] Hollweck (1854-1926) identified this concept of St. Ambrose, "*Poena criminis ex tempore legis,*" with the principle *nulla poena sine lege.*[13]

Pope Gregory the Great in 599 had established the principle of non-retroactivity in ecclesiastical law in his decree *Cognoscentes.*[14] In his commentary on this decree, Hostiensis (+1271) interpreted the statement, "*. . . rem quae culpa caret, in damnum vocari non convenit,*" to mean that any act that is lawfully committed cannot afterwards be punished.[15] Bernard of Pavia (+1213) stated that a newly promulgated law touched only future events, and did not imply punishment for past actions which violated the juridic obligations of a later law.[16] Panormitanus (1386-1453) likewise insisted that new penal laws could not be extended to past acts in punishment of those actions that remained no longer in harmony with the subsequent law.[17]

[11] C. 3, C. XXXII, q. 4.

[12] "Bene dicit poena ex tempore, nam culpa ante legem fuit in Cain et Lamech."—*Glossa Ordinaria,* ad c. 3, C. XXXII, q. 4, s.v. *poena.*

[13] "*Poena criminis ex tempore legis,* oder wie die Doktrin sonst sagt: *nullum crimen sine lege poenali.*"—*Die kirchlichen Strafgesetze* (Mainz, 1899), p. 66, n. 5.

[14] "...rem quae culpa caret, in damnum vocari non convenit. Quoties vero novum quid statuitur, ita solet futuris formam imponere, ut multis dispendiis praeterita non commendet; ne detrimentum ante prohibitionem possint ignorantes incurrere, quod eos postmodum dignum est vetitos sustinere."—c. 2, X, *de constitutionibus,* I, 2; Jaffé, n. 1629; cf. also c. 13, X, *de constitutionibus,* I, 2; Potthast, *Regesta Pontificum Romanorum inde ab anno post Christum natum MCXCVIII ad annum MCCCIV* (2 vols., Berolini, 1874-1875), n. 9526 (hereafter cited Potthast).

[15] "Quod legitime factum est, poenam non meretur."—*Glossa Ordinaria,* ad c. 2, X, *de constitutionibus,* I, 2, s.v. *culpa caret.*

[16] *Summa Decretalium* (ed. E. A. Th. Laspeyres, Ratisbonae, 1860), Appendix IV, *Casus Decretalium,* lib. I, tit. 1, c. 2, p. 328.

[17] "Si constitutio aliqua de novo promulgatur, extenditur ad futura tantum punienda... ita quod praeterita non puniat..."—*Commentaria,* ad c. 2, X, *de constitutionibus,* I, 2.

Frison states that this concept regarding penal law was in general use by the fifth century, and that during the middle ages it received extensive elaboration at the hands of the commentators.[18]

ARTICLE IV. THE PROHIBITION OF ANALOGY IN PENAL LAW

The third concept inherent in the axiom *nulla poena sine lege* is the rule which precludes the application of analogy in penal law. Gratian introduced this concept, and it was later developed by the canonical writers of the middle ages until De Luca (1614-1683) in the seventeenth century referred to it as the *"vulgaris et recepta propositio."*[19]

From Roman Law[20] Gratian borrowed a penal norm which he stated as follows: *"Poenae legum interpretatione molliendae sunt potius quam esasperandae."*[21] He elaborated on this concept in his *dictum* with this explanation: *"Atque ideo proprium casum non excedunt... non ad alios casus extendendae."* Hence Gratian required specific provision in law if a penalty was to be inflicted.[22] It is this very concept that gives legal force and life to the principle *nulla poena sine lege.* Ioannes Andreae (1272-1348) declared this to be the *"recepta regula."*[23]

The rules of law promulgated by Pope Boniface VIII (1294-1303) included two rules that embody the spirit of this concept: *"Odia restringi et favores convenit ampliari"*[24] and *"In poenis benignior est interpretatio facienda."*[25] In his gloss on the latter rule, Ioannes Andreae explained:

[18] *The Retroactivity of Law,* The Catholic University of America Canon Law Studies, No. 231 (Washington, D.C.: The Catholic University of America Press, 1946), p. 153.

[19] *Theatrum Veritatis et Iustitiae* (5 vols., Venetiis, 1734), I, *De Beneficiis,* Disc. XXI, n. 19.

[20] D. (48. 19) 42: "Interpretatione legum poenae molliendae sunt potius quam asperandae."

[21] C. 18, D. I, *de poenit.*

[22] *Glossa Ordinaria,* ad c. 18, D. I, *de poenit.,* s.v. *molliendae sunt.*

[23] *In Sextum Decretalium Librum Novella Commentaria* (Venetiis: 1581), Reg. *In poenis,* De Regulis Iuris in VI°, nn. 2-4.

[24] Reg. 15, R. J., in VI°.

[25] Reg. 49, R. J., in VI°.

Et nota quod haec benigna interpretatio fit in multis: primo ex multiplici poena expressa eligimus mitiorem... item quia verbum potest importare poenam perpetuam et temporalem, eligimus temporalem... item, quia de poenis non arguimus ad similia: quia poenae non excedunt proprium casum...item in dubio mitiorem casum eligimus.[26]

A few cases taken from the sources illustrate the practical application of the concept during the middle ages. During the pontificate of Nicholas III (1277-1280) there was issued the decretal *Cupientes,* which regulated the designation of bishops to vacant sees that had been reserved to Rome. When the penalties established in the Decretal were extended to cases not expressly indicated, the glossators of the 13th century declared it unlawful: *"In aliis, locum non habeat... grave enim esset tantas poenas vel causas imponere in illo casu non expresso."*[27]

A penal statute of Pope Gregory X (1271-1276) that concerned the qualifications for the office of pastor of a parochial church was ruled inapplicable when extended to a *collegiate* parochial office.[28] Ioannes Andrea in his gloss on this decretal quite simply stated: *"Canon poenalis non debet extendi ultra suos terminos."*[29]

The commentators applied this principle also to the decretal *Saepe Contingit.* This decretal was directed to the Italian episcopate and forbade them to ordain foreign candidates unless a certain procedure had been followed. The glossators discussed the question of the applicability of the penalties as established in this decretal to bishops outside Italy if they contravened the prescripts of this law. Again Ioannes Andreae responded: *"Non vero haec decretalis locum habet, quia poenalis est et sic restringenda: et sic proprium non excedit casum."*[30] Panormitanus referred his readers to the commentary of Ioannes Andreae relative to the principle that forbade the analogical

26 *Glossa Ordinaria,* ad Reg. 49, R. J., in VI°.

27 *Glossa Ordinaria,* ad c. 16, *de electione et electi potestate,* I, 6, in VI°, s.v. *immediata subiectio.*

28 C. 22, *de electione et electi potestate,* I, 6, in VI°.

29 *Glossa Ordinaria, loc. cit.,* s.v. *statutum.*

30 *Glossa Ordinaria,* ad c. 1, *de temporibus ordinationum et qualitate ordinandorum,* I, IX, in VI°.

extension of penal law. The doctrine therein contained he characterized as a *"clarissima, verissima et indubitata sententia."*[31]

In an article that appeared in 1936, Orio Giacchi published the results of his investigation into the historical origins of the principle *nulla poena sine lege.* From the abundant evidence that he found in the canonical sources for the rule that forbade the extension of penal laws by way of analogous application, he concluded that the legislator of the Code could find the basic concepts of the principle in the sources and traditions of the Church's own law. He stated his conclusions thus:

> Non e forse inutile mostrare, contra la opinione dominante, come nell' antica dottrina canonistica. . . e piu specialmente in quella del periodo aureo del diritto canonico, che comprende i secoli XII, XIII, et XIV—si trovino traccie evidenti et secure del principio *nullum crimen sine praevia lege poenali* in quanto piu volte gli antichi canonisti insistono sulla non-applicabilità della estensione analogica in materia penale.[32]

CONCLUSION

The juridic concepts inherent in the principle *nulla poena sine lege* were not developed in any one isolated period of history, nor simply in the minds of a few individuals. It appears that they evolved gradually through the course of centuries, their roots striking deeper ground with the passage of the years. Giacchi pointed out that the sources do not evince a constant and unvarying tradition in the application of these penal concepts; there are periods when these penal concepts developed and flourished with greater vitality, and other periods when they seemed to fall into temporary desuetude.[33] But the fact remains that the fundamental concepts of the principle *nulla poena sine lege* were present in the sources of canonical jurisprudence when the legislator, impelled no doubt by the political temper of the times, canonized the principle in the legislation of the present Code.

[31] *Commentaria,* ad c. 30, X, *de praebendis et dignitatibus,* III, 5, s.v. *qui vero.*

[32] "Precedenti Canonistici del Principio 'nullum crimen sine praevia lege poenali'," *Studi in onore di Francesco Scaduto,* I, 438.

[33] *Loc. cit.*

CHAPTER THREE

FROM THE COUNCIL OF TRENT (1545-1563) TO THE CODE (1918)

ARTICLE I. THE COUNCIL OF TRENT

The legislation formulated by the Tridentine Fathers represented in a limited degree a return to the ancient discipline that had allowed the bishops almost unrestricted penal authority.[1] During the first three centuries the government of the churches was left almost exclusively in the hands of the bishop, who of necessity guided almost every phase of the spiritual and temporal life of his diocese.[2] The exercise of the judicial and coercive powers was the almost exclusive prerogative of the bishop, who likewise judged the fitness of candidates for sacred Orders.[3]

It has been noted that from the fourth century the development of a universal legal system brought with it restrictions and regulations until by the time of Gratian public delicts could be punished only after they had been proved in a judicial trial. Pope Alexander III (1159-1181) attested to the fact that a candidate for sacred Orders who was known to be unfit by reason of an occult crime, but whose guilt was not publicly

[1] "Omnes ecclesiarum praelati... quoscumque saeculares clericos, qualitercumque exemptos, qui alias suae iuridictioni subessent, de eorum excessibus, criminibus et delictis, quoties et quando opus fuerit, etiam extra visitationem, tamquam ad hoc Apostolicae Sedis delegati, corrigendi et castigandi facultatem habeant..."—*Conc. Trident.*, sess. XIV, c. 4.

[2] Hinschius, *Kirchenrecht,* IV, 745.

[3] III Council of Carthage (397), can. 22—Bruns, I, 126; c. 2, D. XXIV. Cf. also cc. 3 and 5, D. XXIV.

known, could not be denied promotion to higher Orders if the candidate insisted.[4] For, as Pirhing (1606-1679) explained:

> Ratio est, quia occulta delicta publice vindicanda non sunt, ideoque etsi quis occulte indignus fit... repelli non potest, quia actus publicae potestatis, vel administrationis, non secundum privatam scientiam administrantis vel iudicis, sed secundum publicam notitiam, et opinionem exerceri debent.[5]

Legislation created at the Council of Trent effected at least a partial return to the ancient discipline that accorded complete authorization to the bishops to determine the fitness of a candidate for Orders, and it empowered them to invoke canonical sanctions against crimes of an occult character.[6] This extrajudicial remedy has become known as *suspensio ex informata conscientia;* this radical departure from canonical procedure which dispensed with the need of issuing previous admonitions, and authorized the immediate infliction of a penalty, was justified in view of the troubled times and the abuses that were directly traceable to the entrance of unworthy men into the ranks of the clergy.[7]

The revolutionary character of this extrajudicial penal remedy was entirely foreign to the conservative tradition of

4 "Ex tenore tuarum litterarum accepimus, quod N. clericus adeo deliquit, quod, si peccatum eius esset publicum, degradaretur ab ordine, quem suscepit, et amplius non posset ad superiores ordines promoveri...Verum tamen, quia peccatum occultum est, si promoveri voluerit, eum non potes nec debes aliqua ratione prohibere."—c. 4, X, *de temporibus ordinationum et qualitate ordinandorum,* I, 11; cf. also c. 17, X, *de temporibus ordinationum et qualitate ordinandorum,* I, 11.

5 *Ius Canonicum Nova Methodo Explicatum* (5 vols., Dilingae, 1674-1678), lib. I, tit. XI, n. 17 (hereafter cited *Ius Canonicum*).

6 "Cum honestius ac tutius sit subiecto, debitam praepositis obedientiam impendendo in inferiori ministerio deservire, quam cum praepositorum scandalo graduum altiorum appetere dignitatem, ei, cui ascensus ad sacros ordines a suo praelato ex quacumque causa, etiam ob occultum crimen, quomodolibet, etiam extraiudicialiter, fuerit interdictus, aut qui a suis ordinibus seu gradibus, vel dignitatibus ecclesiasticis fuerit suspensus, nulla contra ipsius praelati voluntatem concessa licentia de se promoveri faciendo, aut ad priores ordines, gradus, dignitates sive honores restitutio suffragetur."—Conc. Trident., sess. XIV, *de ref.,* c. 1.

7 Pallottini, *Pugna Iuris Pontificii Statuentis Suspensiones extraiudicialiter seu ex Informata Conscientia, et Imperii Easdem obrogare Molientis* (Viennae, 1863), pp. 74-76.

canonical procedure.[8] The subsequent opposition that arose against it subsided neither quickly nor easily. Finally Pope Pius VI (1775-1799) declared this resistance *"falsa, perniciosa, in Tridentinum iniuriosa, iurisdictionis praelatorum Ecclesiae laesiva."*[9]

In view of the extraordinary purpose and nature of this penal statute, the special faculty enacted in canon 2222, §1, can be seen as an extension of the extraordinary penal legislation issued at the Council of Trent. The essential purpose of the suspension *ex informata conscientia* was the creation of a canonical remedy that would enable lawful superiors in the Church to invoke sanctions against crimes that would otherwise remain outside the reach of the ordinary penal procedure. This is the general purpose of the special faculty granted in canon 2222, §1.

An evaluation of the historical relationship that exists between these two canonical provisions must be considered in the light of the vaguely defined principles operative in penal law at the time of the Council of Trent. At that time the constitutive elements of a delict had yet to be authoritatively determined, and the axiom *nulla poena sine lege* with the full force of its implications had not yet become an authentic and crystallized penal principle. The common doctrine of the Church was reflected in the teaching of Pirhing:

> Si denique de poena criminis nihil definitum sit in iure, utrum pecuniaria, vel alia sit imponenda, tum iudicis arbitrio relinquitur quam imponat.[10]

Yet, if the crime was committed in such circumstances that it could not be proved in court, no matter how detrimental

[8] "La regle constante du droit, en effet, c'est que nulla peine ne doit être portée contre quel qu' un tant qu' il n'a pas été' convainçu judiciarement du delit dont on l'accuse."—Bourret, *Des Sentences Ecclésiastiques,* p. 19.

[9] Const. *Auctorem fidei,* 28 aug. 1794,—*Fontes,* n. 475, *Propositiones damnatae XLIX et L;* cf. also S. C. de Prop. Fide, instr. 20 oct. 1884, nn. 6-13—*Collectanea,* n. 1628; *Fontes,* n. 4907. The procedure for the infliction of this suspension as outlined in this Instruction was adopted in the present Code with minor changes. Cf. also S.C. Ep. et Reg., instr. 11 iun. 1880—*Fontes,* n. 2005; *Acta Sanctae Sedis* (41 vols., Romae, 1865-1908), XIII (1880-1881), 324-336 (hereafter cited *ASS*); S. C. de Prop. Fide, instr. a. 1883—*Fontes,* n. 4900; *Collectanea,* n. 1586.

[10] *Ius Canonicum,* lib. V, tit. XXXIII, n. 1.

it was, it could not be punished with a canonical penalty. It was to fill this *lacuna legis* that the suspension *ex informata conscientia* was created as a remedy in law. With the advent of the catalogue of ecclesiastical delicts and penalties as delineated in the Code, the lawful superior would be helpless in the face of serious scandal or of an extraordinarily grave transgression when it arose from the violation of a juridic obligation that did not specify a penalty. It was to provide for this *lacuna legis* that the special faculty as incorporated in canon 2222, § 1, was created in the present common law of the Code.[11]

From the standpoint therefore of the extraordinary character of the Tridentine penal statute which permitted the lawful invoking of sanctions against crimes that normally would have escaped punishment, it can be considered as the canonical precursor of the special authority contained in canon 2222, § 1. On the other hand, canon 2222, § 1, is not essentially a procedural statute directed against occult delicts. It has the more general purpose of providing a remedy in law for the punishment of both public and occult delicts that otherwise would not be subject to the application of any canonical sanction, and the authority which it creates is to be employed in accordance with the rules of procedure as established in the Code.

The extrajudicial remedy that was established by the Council of Trent had been directed primarily against occult crimes; yet in the course of time this process was used against public delicts as well, when moral considerations rendered impossible the proof of the crime in the ordinary judicial procedure. A case in point involved a group of rebellious priests led by Charles Passaglia (1812-1887) in a movement prejudicial to the temporal welfare of the Vatican. This group voiced a demand that the Holy See renounce its claims to temporal possessions in Italy in favor of the State. The priests of this fractious movement were suspended *ex informata conscientia,* and this mode of action was sustained when the

[11] "Authors give suspension *ex informata conscientia* as an example [of canon 2222, § 1.] It illustrates the lawfulness of punishing without previous warning, but often the act that is punished by this special decree is one that the law specifies as punishable."—Ayrinhac-Lydon, *Penal Legislation in the New Code of Canon Law* (New York; Benziger Brothers, 1936), n. 40 (hereafter cited *Penal Legislation*).

issue was submitted to Rome by way of recourse.[12] In another instance the publication in the public press of a series of scandalous articles by a disaffected priest was the occasion of suspension inflicted according to the extrajudical remedy. This action by the bishop of San José was supported upon recourse interposed with the Holy See.[13]

From the first it was recognized that suspension *ex informata conscientia* was an extreme measure that contained the possible occasion of abuse. In great measure however history reveals the salutary rôle that this remedy played, and its adoption by the codifiers vindicates its creation by the Fathers of the Council of Trent. There were periods when its use became an ordinary and not the extraordinary process that had been intended.[14] However, with the codification of ecclesiastical delicts and penalties in the present legislation, this extraordinary and extrajudicial process was restored to its proper place, and the provisions of canon 2222, § 1, were established for the purpose of providing a legal mode of punitive action against transgressors of *non-penal* laws whenever the seriousness of the scandal or of the gravity of the transgression requires an effective penal remedy.

ARTICLE II. EXTRAORDINARY PENALTIES

From the middle ages[15] until the appearance of the present Code the provision for the application of *poenae extraordinariae seu arbitrariae* constituted an integral and important part in the penal system of the Church. Ecclesiastical superiors were authorized to determine and to impose some proportionate penalty in the event of the violation of a law that did not

[12] Cavagnis, *Institutiones Iuris Publici Ecclesiastici,* Pars Secunda Specialis (2. ed., Romae, 1889), p. 43.

[13] S. C. Ep. et Reg., 24 aug. 1884—*AAS, XXVII* (1894-1895), 430.

[14] Murphy, *Suspension ex Informata Conscientia,* The Catholic University of America Canon Law Studies, n. 76 (Washington D. C.: The Catholic University of America, 1932), pp. 13 and 23.

[15] "...si certa exinde poena in canonibus exprimatur, eandum infligas; alioquin ipsos pro delicti qualitate et causae secundum tuum arbitrium punire procures."—c. 4, X, *de officio et et potestate iudicis delegati,* I, 29.

specifically call for the infliction of a penalty.[16] In virtue of canon 6, 5°, this provision is to be considered as abrogated in the present discipline of the Code; nonetheless, from the historical viewpoint, there is a direct functional relationship between the discretionary authority allocated to the subordinate superiors in the application of extraordinary penalties and the special faculty accorded to them in canon 2222, § 1. For the discretionary penal authority that existed in the pre-Code practice has been reduced and restricted within the confines of this one canon of the Code.

The determination of the constitutive elements of a delict by the legislator of the Code answered one of the great problems that had existed in pre-Code penal law. The Church from the earliest times had recognized the distinction between delictual and moral guilt, as it was taught by St. Augustine.[17] However, until the nineteenth century the emphasis in penal law rested on the enumeration rather than on the definition of delicts.[18] During the century before the present Code, canonical writers turned their attention and talents to the *science* of penal law. A systematic and analytic study of the constitutive elements that pertained to the nature of an ecclesiastical delict occupied the interests of the commentators, and in particular they discussed the question relative to what legal or juridical elements were postulated for the emergence of a delict.

D'Annibale (1815-1892) declared that only the external violation of a *penal law* constituted an ecclesiastical delict;[19] Tarquini (1810-1874) defined a delict in the same manner,[20]

16 "Poena extraordinaria autem, seu arbitaria est, quae nulla lege statuto aut consuetudine est definita, sed extra ordinem a iudice imponitur iuxta prudens ac iustum eius arbitrium pro varia delictorum qualitate. Sic in re communis doctorum."—Ferraris, *Prompta Bibliotheca, Canonica, Iuridica, Moralis, Theologica, necnon Ascetica, Polemica, Rubricistica, Historica* (9 vols., Romae, 1885-1899), s.v. *poena*, n. 10 (VI, 217).

17 "Apostolus Paulus, quando elegit ordinandos... non ait: 'Si quis sine peccato est,' (hoc enim si diceret, omnis homo reprobaretur, et nullus ordinaretur), sed ait: 'Si quis sine crimine est' ...Crimen enim est grave peccatum, accusatione et damnatione dignissimam."— c. 1, D. LXXXI.

18 Phillips, *Compendium Iuris Ecclesiastici*, auctum et emendatum ed. F. H. Vering, (3. ed., latinae versionis prima, Ratisbonae, 1875), pp. 359-362.

19 *Summula Theologiae Moralis* (3. ed., vols., Romae, 1888-1892), I, 296.

20 *Iuris Ecclesiastici Institutiones* (4 ed., Romae, 1875), p. 15.

and Wernz (1842-1914)[21] taught that the violation of a law or of a precept that did not contain at least an indeterminate sanction could not be treated as an ecclesiastical delict.[22] Hollweck (1854-1926), who was a member of the pontifical commission for the drafting of a penal code, and whose influence on the fifth book of the Code is most evident, defined a delict as an act or omission connoting a culpable violation of a divine or ecclesiastical law when for such a violation the ecclesiastical law had enacted the threat of punishment.[23] It is this definition of a delict that was enacted in the Code almost *verbatim*.

The history of the development of penal law from the time of the Council of Trent to the present Code manifests a definite trend towards limiting the use of penalties to cases which involved transgressions of penal laws. Many of the more severe canonical sanctions were limited to the violation of specific laws.[24] But most of the canonical writers pointed to the possible use of extraordinary penalties, and taught that the existing trend did not constitute an absolute canonical necessity for the juridical element in the ecclesiastical delict prior to the penal legislation of the Code.

In this connection Hinschius (1835-1898) taught that lawful superiors of the Church always have had the power to invoke canonical sanctions against transgressors of the law, whether or not that law incorporated a penal threat. He further declared that it was difficult to see how the Church could maintain the necessary discipline and achieve its spiritual

21 "Quare practice in omni societate exercitium potestatis coercitivae ita debet ordinari, ut per legem certa crimina castigatione digna notentur iustisque poenis subiiciantur, cetera *plerumque* in foro externo et humano relinquantur impunita."—*Ius Decretalium,* VI, p. 15, footnote 11.

22 *Op. cit.,* VI, 13.

23 "Unter kirchlichem Strafvergehen versteht man zum Unterschied von de Sünde eine äussere Handlung oder Unterlassung, welche in schuldbarer Weise ein gottliches oder kirchliches Gesetz verletzt, dessen Uebertretung im kirchlichen Rechte mit Strafe bedroht ist."—*Die kirchlichen Strafgesetze,* pp. 65-66.

24 S.C.C., *Nominationis et Praesentationis,* 14 febr. 1821— Pallottini, *S., Collectio omnium conclusionum et resolutionum quae in causis propositis apud Sacram Congregationem Cardinalium S. Concilii Tridentini Interpretum prodierunt ab eius institutione anno 1564 ad annum 1860, distinctis titulis alphabetico ordine per materias digesta,* 18 vols., Romae, 1868-1895; Pirhing, *Ius Canonicum,* lib. V, tit. XXXVII, n. 16.

mission without such authority which could inflict adequate penalties in atonement for great scandal and the perpetration of perverse crimes.[25]

Lega (1860-1935) challenged the canonical necessity of the legal element as an essential element for an ecclesiastical delict. He had this to say concerning the doctrine that was proposed by Hollweck and Wernz:

> Quae notio delicti... non adamussim exacta videtur in iure ecclesiastico constituto... in quo lex poenalis non est ita expressa ut punire non valeat actus forsan nulla lege positiva prohibitos[26]...

Lega contended that the doctrine of Hollweck and Wernz was too restrictive to answer to the needs of the penal system of the Church as it then existed. He defended the use of the extraordinary or discretionary penalties as essential to the preservation of order in the Church, and he declared that this need would continue until a systematic and authentic code of penal law appeared that would obviate the necessity for them.[27]

Lega was supported in his teaching by the earlier common doctrine of the commentators. Pirhing (1606-1679) had distinguished between ordinary and extraordinary canonical penalties, and had taught that extraordinary penalties were proportionate sanctions determined and imposed by ecclesiastical superiors whenever a violation of non-penal law was so serious as to require punitive action.[28] Gonzales-Tellez (+ after 1673) had stated that it was the practice to follow the decision of Pope Alexander III (1159-1181),[29] who had authorized the imposition of some just penalty even though the law which was violated did not specify a penalty.[30] Another contemporary author who had taught this same doctrine was Fagnanus (1598-1678); he

25 *Kirchenrecht,* V, 906; cf. also Suarez, *Opera Omnia,* V, *Tractatus de Legibus et Legislatore Deo,* Lib. IV, c. 11, n. 5.

26 *Praelectiones in Textum Iuris Canonici, De Delictis et Poenis* (ed. altera, Romae, 1910), pp. 23-24; cf. also Maschat, *Institutiones Canonicae* (ed. ab Ubaldo Giraldi a S. Cajetano, 4 vols. in 2, Florentiae, 1854), lib. V, tit. II, n. 8.

27 *Loc. cit.*

28 *Ius Canonicum,* lib. V, tit. XXXVII, n. 11.

29 C. 4, X, *de officio et potestate iudicis delegati,* I, 29.

30 *Commentaria Perpetua in Quinque Libros Decretalium* (5 vols. in 4, Venetiis, 1699), lib. I, tit. XXIX, n. 3.

had stated that the use of extraordinary penalties was a well-established practice, and then had added that it was a practice which reflected the opinion of both Hostiensis (+1271) and Ioannes Andreae (+1348).[31]

One of the greatest of the pre-Code canonical writers, Reiffenstuel (1642-1703), indicated the same division between ordinary and extraordinary penalties.[32] However, he warned the superior who determined and inflicted a discretionary penalty that personal feelings and desires could play no part in this judgment;[33] he also noted that the usual practice was to temper the severity of these penalties with mercy and mildness.[34]

Lega found that the pattern for these discretionary penalties came into practice from Roman Law, where provision had been made for *crimina extraordinaria;* this provision established authority for the infliction of a suitable penalty whenever an act or an omission seriously disturbed the public order, and the law had not provided for the imposition of a penalty. Then he added:

> Atqui iure canonico *adhuc* viget huiusmodi systema, quod explicant canonistae et commentatores. . . in iure constituendo, optimum erit si stabiliatur lex poenalis ecclesiastica ordinata ad compescendas, per poenas canonicas, quascumque legum violationes ordinem Ecclesiae socialem deturbantes.[35]

However, Lega defended the usefulness of these extraordinary sanctions in the pre-Code penal system; and although he voiced the hope that a future codification of ecclesiastical penal law would obviate the necessity of such broad discretionary authority in the use of coercive power, nonetheless he conjectured the opinion that the Church in its spiritual work to save souls would always have need of some provision that

31 *Commentaria in Quinque Libros Decretalium* (5 vols., Venetiis, 1709), lib. I, tit. XXXI, c. 13, § *caeterum.*

32 *Ius Canonicum Universum,* Lib. V, tit. XXXVII, n. 5.

33 ". . . non enim arbitrium hic accipitur pro arbitrio libero, et absoluto ac pleno voluntatis, sed pro arbitrio regulato a recta ratione, sive pro arbitrio boni viri. . ."—*Ibid.,* n. 10.

34 *Ibid.,* n. 11.

35 *De Delictis et Poenis,* pp. 22-24.

would efficaciously counteract the harm that resulted from sinful and irresponsible conduct.[36] The legislator of the Code vindicated the opinion of Lega when just such a provision was established in canon 2222, § 1.

An epitome of the doctrine and usage of discretionary penalties in the Church prior to the appearance of the present Code was published in a decision of the Sacred Roman Rota in 1910: it concerned a case in which an extraordinary penalty had been inflicted upon a priest who subsequently had taken recourse against the sentence; the Rota failed to support the appeal of the defendant, and explained:

> Neque dicendum est in casu recursus inefficacis... legem ecclesiasticam non infligere poenam... ac proinde nec Episcopum posse eamdem irrogare cum nulla poena sine lege. Etenim in nostro iure (quidquid sit de legislationibus civilibus) quando lex prohibens actum, poenam non constituit, iudex infligere potest poenam arbitrariam, quae cum gravitate culpae commissae proportionem habeat... ex quo Doctores communiter conclusionem suprapositam deducunt.[37]

When the present legislation of the Code became the authentic and exclusive body of common law for the universal Church on the Feast of Pentecost, 1918, only a vestige of the discretional penal power formerly vested in the hands of ecclesiastical superiors had been retained. The legislator had canonized the axiom *nulla poena sine lege,* but at the same time he had provided that the principle in canon law should be accorded a broad and liberal interpretation that conformed to the needs of a society whose primary aim is supernatural. The special faculty granted in canon 2222, § 1, represents a certain essential residuum of the discretionary penal authority that existed in pre-Code practice. For in the present discipline of the Code the discretionary penal power of this canon becomes operative only and whenever a notable scandal or a specially grave transgression requires the use of a punitive measure that has not been provided specifically in the law.

[36] *Loc. cit.*

[37] S.R.R., *Pharen.* (Iurium et Poenarum), 10 iunii 1910, coram R. P. D. Gulielmo Sebastianelli, dec. XX—*S. Romanae Rotae Decisiones seu Sententiae (ab anno 1909)* (Romae: Typis Vaticanis, 1912-), II (1910), 191 (hereafter cited *Decisiones*); cf. also *AAS,* II (1910), 772.

PART II

CANONICAL COMMENTARY

INTRODUCTION

This canonical study is concerned with the two rules of penal law as found in canon 2222, § 1: the one may be called the ordinary rule, and the other is known as the extraordinary rule. However, both norms stem from one and the same principle: *nulla poena sine praevia sanctione poenali.*

The immediately following chapter will consider the ordinary rule for the application of canonical penalties; this rule of law requires that no sanction be invoked unless there was given a prior warning that threatened a penalty, and notwithstanding this admonition the law was violated.

Subsequent chapters will deal with the extraordinary norm of canon 2222, § 1, which is operative only when a juridic obligation is imposed without a specific penal threat, but this non-penal law or precept has been violated in such a way that the scandal given or the special gravity of the transgression has so injured the common good of society as to require the infliction of some punitive measure. This extraordinary norm of canon 2222, § 1, is a modified application of the principle *nulla poena sine lege;* it provides for a liberal and elastic interpretation of this penal principle, but it neither contradicts nor neutralizes its canonical efficacy, as some jurists have asserted.

The integration of this special faculty as granted in canon 2222, § 1, with the general prescripts of the Code, as well as a discussion of the principal problems of interpretation and application, will constitute the substance of the final three chapters of this study.

CHAPTER FOUR

NULLA POENA SINE PRAEVIA SANCTIONE POENALI

ARTICLE I. CONCEPT OF AN ECCLESIASTICAL DELICT

The material object of all penal law is the delict, and therefore essential to the study of canon 2222, § 1, is a clear understanding of the juridical elements that constitute a delict. It is a problem of canonical analysis to ascertain the precise elements that are required to exist in a human act if there is to accrue to it a delictual imputability which subjects that act to the punitive power of ecclesiastical superiors.

For the most part the term *delict* will be used throughout this commentary, although it is understood that the terms *crime* and *transgression* are synonymous with and can be employed interchangeably for the word *delict.*[1]

A delict is defined in Canon Law as an external and morally imputable violation of a law or a precept to which at least an indeterminate penal sanction is attached.[2] From this definition it is evident that the three constitutive elements in the concept of an ecclesiastical delict are: 1) the objective element (*damnum*); 2) the subjective element (*dolus*); and 3) the legal or juridical element (*lex poenalis*).[3]

[1] "Moderna distinctio in *crimina, delicta, transgressiones* neque in antiquis fontibus, neque in Codice invenitur. Nomina quidem occurrunt, sed cum aliis multis promiscue adhibentur."—Chelodi-Ciprotti, *De Delictis et Poenis* (5. ed., Trento: Libraria Moderna Editrice, 1943), n. 3; Vermeersch-Creusen, *Epitome Iuris Canonici* (3 vols., Vol. III, 5. ed., Mechliniae: H. Dessain, 1936), III, n. 383 (hereafter cited *Epitome*); Wernz-Vidal, *Ius Canonicum* (7 vols. in 8, Romae: Apud Aedes Universitatis Gregorianae, 1923-1938), VII, n. 36; Coronata, *Institutiones Iuris Canonici* (2. ed., 5 vols., Taurini: Marietti, 1939-1947), IV, n. 1638 (hereafter cited *Institutiones*).

[2] Canon 2195.

[3] Roberti, *De Delictis et Poenis*, n. 38; Latini, *Summa Lineamenta Iuris Criminalis Philosophici* (Romae: Marietti, 1924), pp. 65-71 (hereafter cited *Summa Lineamenta*); Salucci, *Il Diritto Penale* (2 vols., Subiaco, 1926-1930), I, 1-3.

The objective element is the *external violation* of a law or a precept. Penal law is not concerned with every moral aberration in the ethical order; it is directed solely against designated juridic obligations whose observance, in the judgment of the lawgiver, is necessary for the preservation of the social order.[4] It has already been noted that the Church from the earliest times distinguished the sinful act from the unlawful.[5] Therefore, while every delict is sinful, not every sin is a delict. Subject to the coercive power of the Church are only those sinful external acts which violate the juridic obligations that have been imposed by the lawful legislative authority.[6] Moreover, the violation must be an *external* one,[7] for the Code accepts the legal axiom *"Cogitationis poenam nemo patitur,"*[8] since it remits the judgment of purely internal human acts either to divine justice or to the sacramental forum.[9]

The subjective element of a delict consists in *moral imputability.* Unlike its status in the civil law, a purely juridic guilt does not suffice to constitute delictual imputability, for the Church does not desire to use its punitive power against those whose acts do not at the same time connote the presence of a grave moral guilt.[10] Therefore there can be no true delict without malice or culpable negligence, either of which postulates all the conditions of knowledge and freedom requisite for moral responsibility.[11] However, when a juridical norm

4 Roberti, *De Delictis et Poenis,* n. 34; Latini, *Summa Lineamenta,* pp. 66-67.

5 "Cum pro delictis suis (peccatores) a Christi corpore separentur."—C. 21, C. XI, q. 3; c. 19, C. XXIII, q. 4; c. 1, D. LXXI; c. 1, D. LXXXI.

6 "Prudens legislator crimina determinat non solum ex damno obiectivo, sed ex periculo sociali, ex difficultate defensionis vel reparationis, ex modo violationis, et aliis huiusmodi. Ita, e.g., non quaelibet lectio librorum prohibitorum crimen constituit (c. 1395 ss.), sed tantum in certis casibus (c. 2318.)"—Roberti, *De Delictis et Poenis,* n. 38.

7 "De manifestis quidem loquimur: secretorum autem et cognitor et iudex est Deus."—C. 11, D. 32.

8 C. 14, D. I, *de poenit.*

9 Canon 2195, § 1.

10 "Iudex punit non delectatione alienae miseriae, quod est malum pro malo, sed dilectione iustitiae, quod est iustum pro iniusto, bonum pro malo."—c. 1, C. XXIII, q. 3.

11 Ayrinhac-Lydon, *Penal Legislation;* Roberti, *De Delictis et Poenis,* n. 38.

has been violated in the external forum, a presumption of moral imputability prevails until the contrary is proved.[12]

The juridical element in a delict is the *canonical penal sanction* attached to the law or the precept. Pre-code canonists were not agreed as to the necessity of this element among the essential elements of a delict. But this discussion was terminated when the legislator of the Code required the prior establishment of at least an undetermined penal sanction as essential to the nature of an ecclesiastical delict. Hence it follows that no canonical penalty can be inflicted unless a *penal law* or its equivalent has been violated. As Salucci observes,[13] there are many grave violations of law that are not punishable as true ecclesiastical delicts. This is a corollary of the principle *nulla poena sine lege,* which, as will be seen, has been canonized in the penal law of the Code, although not destined to follow the rigid pattern that obtains in the secular law.

ARTICLE II. THE JURIDICAL ELEMENT

From the standpoint of the natural law, the introduction of the juridical element in the nature of a delict was not required. For the dictates of the natural law are satisfied whenever the objective and subjective elements (*damnum* et *dolus*) co-exist in a human act, in which case the imposition of a proportionate penalty by a competent authority is justified.[14]

Although no intrinsic necessity requires a previous warning of punishment, it can be said that such a warning is relatively necessary in view of the ever present need to safeguard the fundamental rights of the individual members of society.[15] For, as Vidal (1868-1939) pointed out, the exercise of coercive

12 Canon 2200, § 2.

13 *Il Diritto Penale,* I, 2.

14 "...ex natura rerum enim, ut actus quidam punibilis sit, non requiritur praevia sanctionis poenalis comminatio...sed sufficit ut actus ille revera sit moraliter et socialiter malus...; ratio est, quia quoad omnes actus moraliter et socialiter malos adest fundamentum juridicum potestatis coactivae; ..."—Michiels, *Normae Generales* I, 201.

15 "Principium moderni iuris poenalis: nullum crimen, nulla poena sine lege...non ex intrinseca necessitate, sed ex studio severioris iustitiae."—Chelodi-Ciprotti, *De Delictis et Poenis,* n. 2; Latini, *Summa Lineamenta,* p. 68; Wernz-Vidal, *Ius Canonicum,* VII, n. 31.

power by one person over the natural rights of another is so fraught with danger as to call for all possible safeguards against human error and caprice in the administration of punitive power.[16]

In practice, it is generally admitted that the adoption of the principle *nulla poena sine lege* is beneficial both to the governing authority and the individual members of society.[17] On the one hand, as a deterrent to those who would violate the legal norms of society, it has a preventive value in preserving the public order; and, on the other hand, it safeguards the rights of society by limiting the arbitrary penal powers of the governing authority.[18]

The very definition of an ecclesiastical penalty reflects the restraint with which it should be employed, for a *"privatio alicuius boni"*[19] implies both a negation and an evil. Mindful of this fact, the supreme lawgiver introduces the penal legislation of the Code[20] with an exhortation to ecclesiastical superiors to use patience and kindness rather than penal remedies until the need of more severe measures is manifest. In any case, the proposition that lawful superiors should attempt to punish every infraction of the divine and human law is both impractical and impossible of fulfillment. For such an endeavor would serve only to create a state of chaos and confusion rather than to promote the social order.[21]

Rather, the prudent lawgiver considers carefully the needs of the society for which he is legislating, and guided by sane principles of penal law, promulgates a complete and authorita-

16 "Notio Delicti in Iure Codicis," *Jus Pontificium* (Romae, 1921-1940), I-II (1921-1922), 99, (hereafter cited *Jus Pont.*).

17 Latini, *Summa Lineamenta,* p. 69; Michiels, *De Delictis et Poenis,* I (Lublin, Polonia: Universitas Catholica, 1934), p. 75; Wernz-Vidal, *Ius Canonicum,* VII, n. 47; Salucci, *Il Diritto Penale,* I, 106-107; Noval, "De ratione corrigendi ac puniendi sive in iudicio sive extra iure Codicis J. C.," *Jus Pont.,* III, (1923), 206 (hereafter cited "De Ratione Corrigendi").

18 "Declarationem hanc necessario exigit bonum tum sociale tum privatum, libertas tum civilis tum naturalis."—Latini, *Summa Lineamenta,* p. 167.

19 Canon 2215.

20 Canon 2214, § 2.

21 Wernz, *Ius Decretalium,* I, n. 14; Vermeersch-Creusen, *Epitome,* III, n. 383.

tive catalogue of legal norms subject to punitive action in the event of their violation.[22]

ARTICLE III. "NULLA POENA SINE LEGE" IN CANON LAW

Before the appearance of the Code the canonical validity of the principle contained in the formula *nulla poena sine lege* was a matter of widely divergent opinion.[23] However, the legislator of the Code brought a peremptory halt to this controversy when it was decreed that "... a delinquent may not be punished unless he has first been admonished and threatened with a *latae* or *ferendae sententiae* penalty in the event of a transgression, and nevertheless has violated the law in question."[24] With similar clarity the canonization of this principle appears in the very first canon of the penal code, where the lawgiver declares that no violation of an ecclesiastical law or precept can be punished unless "... at least an undetermined canonical sanction has been attached."[25]

The extensive abrogation contained in canon 6, 5°, in effect verifies the adoption of this principle in the law of the Code. For there have been abolished not only all the penalties that stand contrary to the law of the Code, but also all the penalties of which the Code no longer makes express mention. Consequently, silence in respect to any particular penalty argues its abrogation, and it must accordingly be regarded as abolished. "One may conclude," Cicognani observes, "from the meaning

22 "Legislatoris est, praesupposito abstracto illo vere philosophico et iuridico principio de puniendis illis solis actionibus, quae ordinem socialem perturbant aut in discrimen adducunt, inter variarum legum transgressiones, illas deligere, quas ductus sanis principiis politicae criminalis, merito reputare debet eas esse tales, quae, attento fine societatis, natae sint illam perturbationem socialem inducere, ideoque munienda sint antecedenter sanctione poenali, qua arceantur subditi a tali transgressione... et si, comminatione non obstante, exoriatur transgressio et consequens socialis ordinis turbatio, ordo laesus restauretur inflicto malo poenae, quo simul efficacia comminationis omnibus intimetur in finem publicae securitatis."—Vidal, "Notio Delicti in Iure Codicis," *Jus Pont.*, I-II (1921-1922), 100.

23 D'Annibale, *Summula Theologiae Moralis*, I, p. 296; Hollweck, *Die kirchlichen Strafgesetze*, pp. 65-66; Wernz, *Ius Decretalium*, VI, n. 16; Lega, *De Delictis et Poenis*, pp. 23-24; Tarquini, *Institutiones Iuris Ecclesiastici Publici*, n. 25; S. R. R., *Pharen.* (*Iurium et Poenarum*), 10 iun. 1910, coram R. P. D. Gulielmo Sebastianelli, dec. XX—*Decisiones*, II (1910), 191; *AAS*, II (1910), 772.

24 Canon 2222, § 1: "...secus reus puniri nequit..."

25 Canon 2195, §§ 1 and 2.

of Canon 6, 5°, that the Code has approved the frequently quoted adage 'nullum crimen, nulla poena sine lege'."[26]

Throughout the Fifth Book of the Code, the constant insistence of the legislator that ecclesiastical delicts and penalties are terms of one and the same equation serves to verify this same conclusion.[27] This inter-dependence between the canonical delict and the ensuing penalty, which is the basis of the principle *nulla poena sine lege,* is most evident in canons 2195, 2215, and 2233, § 1.

Notwithstanding these facts, there are those who agree with Fedele who denies the validity of this principle in Canon Law as well as its corollary rule that prohibits analogous interpretation in penal law.[28] According to this author, the one supreme motive in the law of the Code is the *favor animarum;* to this consideration all other canonical principles are subordinated,[29] and to it, every ecclesiastical guarantee of individual rights and liberties is sacrificed.[30]

The practical consequences of this one all-important consideration, according to Fedele, are far-reaching. Ecclesiastical penal law is no longer considered as a *res odiosa* but rather as a *res favorabilis,* and therefore subject to the ordinary legal rules of interpretation. In the absence of a penal law, an ecclesiastical judge not only has the right but the obligation to fill in this lacuna if "...il *periculum animarum* venga in considerazione."[31] For the same reason, the extension of penal law by analogy is not unlawful when the violation of a non-penal law is considered.[32]

26 *Canon Law* (2. rev. ed., authorized English version by J. O'Hara F. Brennan, Westminister, Md.: The Newman Bookshop, 1946), p. 506.

27 Latini, *Summa Lineamenta,* p. 203.

28 "Stando così le cose, è chiaro che il divieto dell' analogia nell'interpretazione della legge penale e il principio *nullum crimen sine praevia lege poenali* non trovano applicazione nell'ordinamento canonico."—*Discorso Generale sull'Ordinamento Canonico* (Padova: Cedam, 1941), n. 38, p. 88.

29 "...un motivo superiore...che consiste nell'idea ultraterrena della salvezza delle anime e che, transformando la legge penale da *odiosa* in *favorabilis*—a cagione del *favor animarum*—rende possible l'applicazione in materia penale delle ordinarie regole di interpretazione della legge."—*Op. cit.,* p. 98.

30 "...nel diritto della Chiesa manca ogni idea di garanzie connesse ai soggetti di diritto contro gli organi della Chiesa stessa dotati di potere punitivo;..."—*Op. cit.,* p. 99.

31 *Op. cit.,* p. 98.

32 *Op. cit.,* p. 99.

The present writer does not presume to undertake a detailed criticism of this article except to point out briefly that in his opinion it is both faulty and misleading. It is true, as Fedele asserts, that the *lex suprema* of the Church is the *salus animarum;* upon this premise the common law of the Code was *formulated.* But to deny the valid application of the specific prescripts and principles contained in the Code because of this one supreme motive is to misunderstand the supernatural mission of the Church and its constant concern to render justice and equity to its individual subjects.

It is because of this one supreme motive, and not in spite of it, that the lawgiver definitely adopted the principle *nulla poena sine lege*[33] along with its consequent corollary which rejects all analogous interpretation in penal matters.[34] This is an inescapable conclusion from canon 20[35] where the legislator provides for supplementary legislation. It is evident that no body of law could attempt to set up legal norms for every possible course of action; therefore the lawgiver directs that subordinate superiors have recourse to four different sources of ecclesiastical jurisprudence as a canonical means of supplying for any possible *lacuna legis.* However canon 20 carefully and specifically withholds this authority whenever it involves the application of penalties. This is in strict conformity with the canonical adoption of the principle *nulla poena sine lege.* Penal law is to be interpreted as a *res odiosa,* subject to strict interpretation,[36] and applied in the light of the benign rule of canon 2219, § 1: *in poenis benignior est interpretatio facienda.*[37]

[33] Canons 6, 5°; 10; 2195; 2215; 2222, § 1.

[34] Canon 2219, § 3. Non licet poenam de persona ad personam vel de casu ad casum producere, quamvis par adsit ratio, imo gravior...

[35] Si certa de re desit expressum praescriptum legis sive generalis sive particularis, norma sumenda est, *nisi agatur de poenis applicandis...* (Italics inserted).

[36] Canon 19; cf. Van Hove, *De Legibus Ecclesiasticis* (Mechliniae: Dessain, 1930), c. 19.

[37] "Suprema regula est: 'In poenis benignior est interpretatio facienda ...' Quae tum in dubio iuris, an lex existat aut ad illum casum se extendat (can. 6, 5° et can. 15), tum in dubio facti, an delictum sit certum et perfectum, locum habet. Unde in poenalibus non admittitur analogia (can. 20), neque productio de persona in personam vel de casu ad casum, quamvis par adsit ratio, imo gravior."—Chelodi-Ciprotti, *De Delictis et Poenis,* n. 23.

It seems that those who share the opinion expressed by Fedele mistakenly apply this supreme consideration—the *favor animarum*—as the over-riding rule of penal interpretation, with the result that the positive prescripts of the Code in some cases are distorted. Indubitably the salvation of souls is the sovereign and motivating cause in the *formulation* of all ecclesiastical legislation. This fact, however, does not permit the subsequent interpretation of the positive principles and prescripts of the Code in a way that does violence to the usual and obvious meaning of their text.[38]

The general penal norm of canon 2222, § 1, which requires that a delinquent receive a specific threat of a penalty before the penalty is imposed, applies to all juridic obligations, no matter what form they take. However, if the law threatens a *latae sententiae* penalty, it is clear that the threat as postulated in canon 2222, § 1, is verified through the constant warning given in the law itself.[39]

The law makes no distinction between vindicative and medicinal penalties, and therefore the principle applies to both types of canonical sanctions.[40] However, the principle does operate differently in relation to these two canonical penalties. A vindicative sanction has the primary purpose of punishment for the delict.[41] To inflict a threatened *ferendae sententiae* penalty of this type it suffices to establish that a grave and morally imputable violation has occurred. But for the inflicting of a threatened *ferendae sententiae* censure something more is required; for a censure, whose primary purpose is of a corrective nature, presupposes a contempt for the law itself and the authority behind it. This element of contumacy must be present, and to establish this fact it is necessary to admonish the delinquent; only if this special admonition proves ineffective can the subsequent infliction of the censure lawfully

38 Canon 18.

39 Canon 2217 and 2242, § 2.

40 "...praeviis monitionibus, et comminatione poenae ante violationem legis aut praecepti, quae iure Codicis, c. 2222, § 1, requiruntur non modo pro poenis medicinalibus, ut iure veteri, sed, extra casum specialis scandali vel transgressionis, pro quibuslibet poenis etiam vindicativis, cum legislator ibi dicat indiscriminatim..."—Noval, "De Ratione Corrigendi," *Jus Pont.*, III (1923), 206.

41 Canon 2286.

follow.[42] Thus, if a cleric is unlawfully absent from his residential benefice, his ordinary should warn him to return before a certain date under threat of suspension; if the delinquent has not by that date complied the penalty can be imposed immediately.

In secular law the juridical element of a delict ordinarily is restricted to one form: the penal law. This is not true in canon law, for here it assumes various forms. The reason for this is found in the essential difference that exists between a religious and a secular society.[43] In the Church the governing authority can be called a hierarchial monarchy.[44] Such a constitution endows its lawful superiors with a unified authority, with the result that legislative, executive and judiciary powers are not divided into three separate and distinct branches, as is the case in the modern republican form of civil government. The result is that the ecclesiastical superior with ordinary power not only can enact laws but also can attach penalties to them. Thus the bishop of a diocese is empowered to enact a penalty for the violation of a law of the Code, which penalty is validly constituted as law within the limits of his jurisdiction, but elsewhere lacks all validity as a penal law; and if the needs of his region require it, he is empowered to intensify the penal sanctions that have been constituted in the common law of the Code.[45]

The various forms in which the juridical element of an ecclesiastical delict may appear are usually grouped into four classes:[46] 1) a penal law, promulgated either for the universal Church or as a particular law; 2) a penal precept,[47] issued by a competent superior to individual subjects as a personal law; 3) a canonical admonition, by means of which some existing obligation is urged under the threat of some penalty;[48] 4) a

42 Canon 2233, §§ 1 and 2.

43 Coronata, *Institutiones*, IV, n. 1638.

44 Ottaviani, *Compendium Iuris Publici Ecclesiastici*, nn. 126-129; Wernz-Vidal, *Ius Canonicum*, VII, n. 32.

45 Canon 2221.

46 Roberti, *De Delictis et Poenis*, n. 54.

47 Canons 24; 2195, § 2.

48 Canons 2222, § 1, 2233, § 2; 2242, § 2; 2310.

non-penal preceptive norm, if its violation is attended with notable scandal or a special gravity.[49]

No matter what form the juridical element may assume in ecclesiastical law, the principle if not the formula *nulla poena sine lege* operates as a canonical guarantee for the rights of the individual faithful. It is true that the formula itself is not adequate to meet the canonical provisions in penal law, and it should be modified to read thus: *nulla poena sine praevia sanctione poenali,* which as a more comprehensive formula embraces the four classifications enumerated above.[50]

One must note in passing that the provision in canon 2222, § 1,with reference to cases of serious scandal and of specially grave transgressions does not neutralize the efficacy of this canonical principle, as some have affirmed.[51] Subsequent articles will treat this problem more extensively; for the present, suffice it to say that this special provision of canon 2222, § 1, assumes the character of a general penal law, which threatens with an undetermined penal sanction the violations of non-penal norms in the exceptional and occasional case wherein the scandal given or the accompanying gravity of the transgression transcends the ordinary degree of malice.

Clearly this canon provides the juridical element that permits such violations to be treated as true ecclesiastical delicts.[52] To those who feel that such a provision dissipates the real efficacy of the general principle, these two points should be kept in mind: first, delictual imputability obtains in these cases *only* when the given scandal or the gravity of the transgression is extraordinarily grave, so that unless this essential condition is fulfilled, the special authority is withheld; and, secondly, this canon does not create juridic obligations nor does it establish any retroactive penal law. Canon 2222, § 1, relates only to

[49] Canon 2222, § 1.

[50] Michiels, *De Delictis et Poenis,* p. 77.

[51] "...il superiore ecclesiastico avesse facoltà di reprimere il delitto, onde evitare lo scandalo da esso derivante, anche in mancanza di una disposizione legislativa che contemplasse il delitto o la sua repressione... e per convincersi di ciò basta leggere la singolare disposizione del can. 2222, §1, che suona così: 'Licet lex nullam sanctionem appositam habeat...'."—Fedele, *Discorso Gênerale sull'Ordinamento Canonico,* p. 99.

[52] Canon 2195.

laws (*"Licet lex. . ."*) that do not incorporate a specific threat of a canonical penalty. No authority is granted in virtue of this canon to punish the emergence of scandal except in relation to the violation of existing juridic norms. It is the opinion of this writer that the principle *nulla poena sine praevia sanctione poenali* was adopted by the legislator of the Code with a view to making it consistently operative throughout all ecclesiastical legislation without exception.

ARTICLE IV. "NULLA POENA SINE LEGE" IN SECULAR LAW

From the time of the French Revolution this principle has been enshrined in almost every modern secular penal code. At least in theory no exception to this principle is tolerated in the infliction of legal penalties, and, as Michiels points out, it would be a mistake not to recognize that secular law accords the principle a much more rigid interpretation than it receives in ecclesiastical law.[53]

The modern republican form of civil government was created in an atmosphere of basic distrust of authority and under the fear of tyranny. This attitude is reflected in the political system which sharply divides the sovereign authority into the three conventional departments, and suffers no interference from one department in the powers allocated to another.

Essentially, however, sovereign authority is indivisible. The power to enact a law radically implies the authority to judge the violations of law and to enforce observance with penalties if necessary.[54] The hierarchical monarchy of the Church recognizes this unity of authority, and hence the ecclesiastical superior with ordinary power of jurisdiction is authorized to enact penal laws and precepts, to judge the viola-

[53] "Maxime tamen erraret, qui crederet in his canonis verbis authentice sanciri principium 'nullum crimen, nulla poena sine lege poenali praevia,' sensu rigorosissimo et absoluto, quo principium istud intelligitur et applicatur in juribus saecularibus hodiernis."—*De Delictis et Poenis,* p. 76

[54] "The rule is that coercive power follows legislative power; for even though we may distinguish sovereignty into the three well-known departments, legislative, judiciary and coercive, radically and virtually they must be held by one and the same sovereign power... therefore the Code says that those who enjoy legislative power are authorized to attach a penal sanction to their laws. . ."—Augustine, *A Commentary on the New Code of Canon Law* (8 vols., St. Louis: Herder, 1918-1922), VIII, 82-83.

tions that occur, and to inflict lawful penal sanctions. Such authority of course is impossible in any political system that divides sovereignty into three distinct departments.

To a large extent this fact explains the broad and liberal interpretation with which the principle is applied in canon law in contrast to the strict interpretation of the secular law. To explain this contrast more fully, it is necessary to remember that the ultimate guide in the *formulation* of all ecclesiastical law is the salvation of souls. While the Church is legislating for eternal values, the chief concern of the State is with temporalities, where even extraordinary scandal and very serious transgressions of the law are allowed at times to pass with impunity in the interests of preserving the strict interpretation of the principle *nulla poena sine lege.*

Those who unfavorably compare the liberal construction accorded this principle in Canon law with the strict interpretation of the secular courts would do well also to compare the relatively brief and concise penal code of canon law with the unwieldy penal codes of the modern state. For this strict interpretation of the principle in civil law has given rise to the necessity of legislating for every minute detail of municipal, state and federal life. The annual addition of hundreds of statutes has rendered difficult, if not impossible, the observance of the legal axiom: *ignorantia legis neminem excusat.*

It is interesting to note that even the secular law finds it necessary, in practice, to mitigate the severity of its legal theory concerning the application of this principle. A case in point is the situation that was created by the War Criminal Trials that followed World War II, when of necessity the strict interpretation of this principle was temporarily abandoned. But much to the chagrin of the lawyers who conducted the trials, it could be relegated only to the background, where it still cast a pall of doubt over the legality of the entire proceedings.

As a matter of fact, there are few if any penal codes that do not contain a substitute, in some form or other, for the special provision contained in canon 2222, § 1. Frequently these civil law catch-alls take such vague and elusive forms as "disturbing the peace" or "loitering;" then again legal loopholes are employed in the inflicting of penalties for those transgressions of law that otherwise could not be punished. A case in point is the Federal Income tax law that frequently has been used as the secular law counterpart to the special faculty, for the use of which canon 2222, § 1, makes due legal provision.

The truth of the matter may lie in the fact that every penal code needs a general penal law similar to the special faculty contained in canon 2222, § 1, for as Seagle points out:

> For use against the enemies of a state who are comprised in the classifications of 'radicals,' 'trouble-makers,' and 'labor agitators,' the prosecutor has his blunderbusses. These consist of such vague crimes as 'disorderly conduct,' 'crimes against public morals,' and the like... No penal code has ever been able to get along without at least a few omnibus offenses, *nulla poena sine lege* to the contrary notwithstanding.[55]

The legislator of the Code recognized that a strict and inflexible interpretation of the principle *nulla poena sine lege* did not meet the needs of a society whose mission on earth is supernatural. And therefore the special authority as vindicated in canon 2222, § 1, tempers the rigidity of the principle in order to provide a canonical remedy for transgressions of law that involve a special scandal or gravity.

[55] Seagle, *The Quest for Law* (New York: Alfred Knopf, 1941), c. 16, p. 247.

CHAPTER FIVE

THE EXTRAORDINARY PENAL FACULTY ENACTED IN CANON 2222, § 1

ARTICLE I. AN APPARENT CANONICAL ANTINOMY

It has been seen in the previous chapter that the principle *nulla poena sine praevia sanctione poenali* was canonized by the codifier as a basic and fundamental norm to guide the lawful ecclesiastical superior in the exercise of his coercive power. The unequivocal and explicit expression of this principle is found in the very first canon of the penal code,[1] where it is stated that no ecclesiastical delict exists unless it involves the violation of a law to which at least an undetermined canonical sanction has been added. The consistant application of the principle is found throughout the Code where the terms *delictum* and *poena* are employed only as terms of one and same equation.[2]

A reaffirmation of this principle is contained in the canon which is the object of this study;[3] but this canon also contains a provision that dispenses the lawful superior in certain exceptional cases from the need of issuing a specific warning before inflicting an ecclesiastical penalty.[4] Herein lies a seeming contradiction of canonical norms.

The special faculty enacted in this canon authorizes lawful ecclesiastical superiors to invoke some just and equitable penal sanction against a delinquent who had no other knowledge, apart from the warning contained in this canon itself, that the transgression of a particular juridical norm was subject to punishment. This seeming derogation from the general norm

1 Canon 2195.

2 Canons 2215; 2222, § 1; 2233, § 1.

3 Canon 2222, § 1: "...secus reus puniri nequit..."

4 Canon 2222, § 1: "...etiam sine praevia poenae comminatione..."

is authorized only in cases where some exceptional gravity in the transgression or some notable scandal is involved.[5] In the absence of this extraordinary element the disposition of the law does not operate.

It is evident that the antimony which appears to exist between the principle *nulla poena sine praevia sanctione poenali* as enunciated in canon 2195 and the special faculty authorized in canon 2222, § 1, is only apparent, so that a real contradiction in principles does not obtain.[6] Both canonical norms proceed from one and the same lawgiver, and thus there is precluded the possibility of a real conflict in principle.

At this point the present writer desires to signalize his doctrine that the problem envisions not two contradictory principles, but in reality there is involved two variant applications of one and the same principle: *nulla poena sine praevia sanctione poenali.* Canon 2222, §1, gives expression to two coordinate norms of penal law for the infliction of canonical penalties, both norms being in full harmony with the one prevailing principle.[7]

In the interests of clarity, the distinction can be made between the ordinary norm and the extraordinary norm: the ordinary norm of procedure in the infliction of canonical penalties is concerned with the violation of those laws and precepts in which is contained an express threat of a penalty even though in some cases as an undetermined penalty it is still to receive its ultimate specification; the extraordinary norm[8] has as its exclusive province all those laws and precepts in which no mention whatsoever is made of a penalty in the event of a violation.

[5] Canon 2222, § 1: "...si scandalum forte datum aut specialis transgressionis gravitas id ferat; ..."

[6] Il contenuto della questione sostanziale è dato dai can. 2195 e 2222, § 1, che sembrano essere in contradizione... quei due canoni... non costituiscono contradizione... possono e devono concordarsi. Ma come?"—D'Angelo, "Nozione del Delitto nel Codice di Diritto Canonico," *Ephemerides Theologicae Lovanienses* (Lovanii, 1924-), III (1926), 211 (hereafter cited "Nozione del Delitto," *ETL*).

[7] "Huic principio de necessitate elementi iuridici non opponitur can. 2222, sed potius illud firmat."—Wernz-Vidal, *Ius Canonicum,* VII, n. 34.

[8] "Che tale caso di retroattività poi debba concepsirsi come *eccezione...* e evidentissimo."—D'Angelo, "Nozione del Delitto," *ETL,* III (1926), 217.

The need of a solution for the apparent antinomy that exists between canon 2195 and canon 2222, § 1, is evident. In order that any explanation be acceptable, it must be based on the major premise that the lawgiver has canonized the principle *nulla poena sine praevia sanctioni poenali* and at the same time,[9] under certain circumstances, has made provision for the infliction of penalties *"etiam sine praevia poenae comminatione."*[10] For neither of these two canonical provisions can be rejected without doing violence to the express prescripts of the Code.

An exposition and evaluation of the various theories offered with a view to integrating and harmonizing canon 2195 and canon 2222, § 1, will follow in the next two articles.

ARTICLE II. THEORIES OF CONCORDANCE

Efforts on the part of canonists to resolve the apparent antinomy that exists between the prescripts of canon 2195 and canon 2222, § 1, have produced various theories which can be grouped roughly under four categories. These four schools of thought have approached the problem with the fundamental presumption that no real contradiction in principle exists inasmuch as both canons have one and the same author. All four interpretations have merit to the extent that they harmonize and integrate the prescripts of the two canons without doing violence to any express provision of the Code.

This is not to say that all have equal value; for, as will be pointed out, a concordance of real merit is not attained by ignoring the difficulty or by violating, if not the letter, at least the spirit of the law. It is the opinion of this writer that only one interpretation offers a consistent expression of the mind of legislator. A brief summary of the four theories will follow, with a discussion of their relative merit.

A. The Transgression Theory

According to this explanation, there is a canonical distinction between a delict and a transgression.[11] This opinion is based on the fact that canon 2195 deals exclusively with true

9 Vidal, "Notio Delicti in Iure Codicis," *Jus Pont.*, I, 101.

10 Canon 2222, § 1.

11 Vermeersch-Creusen, *Epitome*, III, n. 383; Muñiz, *Procedimientos Eclesiásticos* (2. ed., 3 Vols., Sevilla, 1925), III, n. 544.

ecclesiastical delicts, and that canon 2222, § 1, is concerned with *transgressions* of law. This theory insists that the constitutive elements of a delict are set forth in canon 2195 and permits no relaxation; however, the special authority granted in canon 2222, § 1, is designed for the punishment of certain serious transgressions of non-penal law in exceptional cases.

This distinction between delicts and transgressions is commonly found in the penal codes of the secular law;[12] in such cases the delict involves an intrinsic evil, and a transgression is evil solely for the reason that a prohibiting law has been violated.[13] While it is true that the secular law does distinguish between delicts and transgressions, it is equally true that the Code does not employ this distinction.[14] The term *transgressio* is used in the Code but four times: in canons 2222, § 1; 2242, § 2; 2310; and 2312, § 2.[15] It is obvious that the use of the word "transgression" in both canon 2242, § 2, and canon 2310 has synonymous value with the term "delict," and is linked with the infliction of canonical penalties in full compliance with the requirements of canon 2195. It is true that canon 2312, § 2, appears to distinguish between delicts and transgressions; but this canon is concerned not with canonical penalties, but with penances.

While this opinion cannot be branded as untenable, it is devoid of a canonical *fundamentum in re,* and as a solution for the difficulty it is acceptable only to those who close their eyes to the real problem involved.

B. The Rule and Exception Theory

The protagonists of this theory[16] argue that the lawgiver promulgates a general rule in canon 2195, and in canon 2222,

12 "I reati si distinguono in delitti e contravvenzione."— Article 39, *Codex poenalis italicus;* Coronata, *Institutiones,* IV, n. 1639.

13 Roberti, *De Delictis et Poenis,* n. 42.

14 "Codex noster non solum non admittit distinctionem inter crimen et delictum sed nec inter delictum et transgressionem."—Coronata, *Institutiones,* IV, n. 1638; Chelodi-Ciprotti, *De Delictis et Poenis,* n. 3; Roberti, *De Delictis et Poenis,* n. 43.

15 Lauer, *Index Verborum Codicis Iuris Canonici* (Typis Polyglottis Vaticanis, 1941), p. 623.

16 Chelodi-Ciprotti, *De Delictis et Poenis,* nn. 2, 25; Sole, *De Delictis et Poenis* (Romae: Pustet, 1920), nn. 6, 85; Salucci, *Il Diritto Penale, I,* 105-109.

§ 1, provides for an obvious exception to that rule.[17] It is evident, they say, that the two rules of law are in complete contrast to each other and that they must be interpreted in the sense that canon 2222, § 1, reflects an exception to the general rule.[18] Salucci contends that the lawgiver who can legislate a general rule can also qualify it with an exception if it is deemed necessary in the interests of the common good.[19] The exponents of this solution offer no apology for this exception to the general rule; they point to the natural law itself which does not demand the juridical element as essential to the nature of a delict, and they emphasize the pre-Code practice which allowed the occasional infliction of ecclesiastical penalties apart from any previous warning. As Sole contends:

> Nam violatio legis, si reapse sit societati noxia, adsit nempe scandalum, quamvis desit praevia legis constitutio, criminis notam et consequenter onus poenae effugere nequit.[20]

It is the opinion of the present writer that the exponents of this theory are victims of the temptation to over-simplify what in fact is a rather intricate problem in canonical exegesis. It is true that the lawgiver has the authority to modify any general principle; but an exception is not presumed. The presumption against such exceptions prevails until the contrary is proved. In this case, as Roberti mentions,[21] the latitude of the exception would be so great that for all practical purposes the efficacy of the general principle would be nullified.

The argument for this "rule and exception" theory from the standpoint of the natural law and the pre-Code practice is of doubtful value in seeking a satisfactory solution for the

17 "Questo canone costituisce una vera e propria eccezione alle regole generali del diritto penale."—Salucci, *Il Diritto Penale,* I, 105.

18 "...praevia declaratio seu constitutio legis poenalis in iure ecclesiastica non ita absolute et taxative exigitur, ut si desit, delictum numquam haberi queat."—Sole, *De Delictis et Poenis,* n. 85.

19 "Che se la Chiesa di un principio generale ne ha fatto una eccezione, ciò depende dal suo giusto criterio di prudenza, secondo la quale è non solo opportuno, ma necessario fissare delle norme, specie in fatto di diritto penale."—*Il Diritto Penale,* I, 105-106.

20 Sole, *De Delictis et Poenis,* n. 85.

21 *De Delictis et Poenis,* n. 51.

apparent contradiction. The primary function of all positive human law is the perfection and completion of the natural law; this function is fulfilled in canon 2195 where the constitutive elements of a delict are determined. This canonical determination of the elements of a delict was lacking in the pre-Code law, and consequently the occasional infliction of an ecclesiastical penalty apart from any previous warning was justified. But the acceptance of the principle *nulla poena sine praevia sanctione poenali* in the Code removes the applicability of an argument based on the pre-Code practice.

The canonical writers who adhere to this opinion emphasize the contrast between the general rule that requires at least an indeterminate sanction in the penal law and the exception of canon 2222, § 1. However, as will be seen in the next article, the contrast is not so pronounced as a cursory reading of the two canons may indicate; under careful analysis the contrast disappears when through an integrated study of the two canons one notes that their rules proceed from one and the same canonical principle.

C. The Theory of Retroactivity

The proponents of this interpretation[22] adduce the principle of the occasional retroactivity of penal law with a view to eradicating the seeming conflict between the rules contained in canons 2195 and 2222. This theory rests on the premise that the principle *nulla poena sine lege* has been canonized in canon 2195, where the necessity of the juridical element in an ecclesiastical delict has been established in an absolute way. But these authors recognize in canon 2222, § 1, a bestowal of authority for the enacting of penalties with retroactive effect.[23]

[22] D'Angelo, "Nozione del Delitto," *ETL*, III (1926), 210-218; Maroto, *Institutiones Iuris Canonici ad Normam Novi Codicis* (2 vols., Vol. I, 2 ed., Madrid, 1919), I, n. 184; Cicognani, *Canon Law*, pp. 506, 555; De Meester, *Juris Canonici et Juris Canonico-Civilis Compendium* (nova editio, 3 vols. in 4, Brugis: Desclée de Brouwer et Soc., 1921-1928), III, pars secunda, p. 144, footnote n. 4; Bouscaren-Ellis, *Canon Law* (Milwaukee: Bruce Publishing Co., 1946), p. 25.

[23] "...Dal can. 2222, § 1, invece, si deduce la possibilità in diritto canonico d' una eventuale *retroattività* della legge o del precetto penale, resi tali della sanzione che si applica."—D'Angelo, "Nozione del Delitto," *ETL*, III (1926), 213.

D'Angelo (1885-1930) traced the historical development of the principle of retroactivity as borrowed from the Roman Law and obtaining in the pre-Code law, from which by way of a natural transition it passed into the law of the Code, where it finds expression in the special penal authority as granted in canon 2222, § 1. According to D'Angelo, it is not canon 2222, §1, that has retroactive force, but it is in virtue of the authority granted in this canon that the act of the lawful superior who enacts and inflicts the penalty becomes invested with retroactive force. The infliction of a canonical penalty for the violation of a non-penal law or precept changes its character from a mere prohibiting law to a penal law.[24] Thus a harmony is established between the two canons and no compromise of the principle *nulla poena sine praevia sanctione poenali* is in any way necessitated.

It is true that this theory does not violate the letter of the common law of the Code, and as such it offers indeed a tenable solution; but it is the opinion of this writer that it fails to offer a *satisfactory* solution which truly reflects the mind and intent of the lawgiver.

The principle of retroactivity is essentially odious; as a principle it is completely foreign to the tenor of the Church's penal code, in which the supreme rule of interpretation is: "In poenis benignior est interpretatio facienda."[25] A general rejection of this principle is set forth in the first book of the Code,[26] and this principle of non-retroactivity is in turn complemented through the adoption of the principle of penal retroactivity *in mitius,* which requires that the milder of any two possible sanctions be invoked.[27] From this it appears that if retroactivity resolves the apparent antinomy between canon 2195 and canon 2222, § 1, its place would be taken immediately by several other canonical conflicts, which in principle would

24 "Quello che rende penale la legge gia esistente non è dunque tutto il can. 2222, § 1, ...ma lo stesso atto del legittimo Superiore, ossia la stessa applicazione della pena con quell'effetto retroattivo su ricordato."—D'Angelo "Nozione del Delitto," *ETL,* III (1926), 217.

25 Canon 2219, § 1.

26 Canon 10. Leges respiciunt futura, non praeterita, nisi nominatim in eis de praeteritis caveatur.

27 Canon 2226, § 2: "...applicanda est lex reo favorabilior."

present no less difficulty for a harmonious solution than the problem at hand.

The use of the principle of an occasion retroactivity in the Roman Law and in the pre-Code practice was regarded by D'Angelo as evincing the natural transition of the principle into the Code. The fact is that the adoption of the principle *nulla poena sine lege* in any penal code strikes directly at the evils inherent in the principle of penal retroactivity. No such bulwark against retroactivity existed in the Roman Law or in the pre-Code law or practice, but, as D'Angelo agreed, *nulla poena sine lege* is a fundamental principle in the penal law of the Code.[28]

For all practical purposes it is impossible to contain in one and the same penal code the principle *nulla poena sine lege* along with the principle of retroactively applicable penalties. For, as Roberti points out,[29] the acceptance of the theory of retroactive penal sanctions is tantamount to the rejection of the necessity of the juridical element in an ecclesiastical delict. Perhaps D'Angelo had this difficulty in mind when he wrote:

> È qui l'errore fondamentale... di considerare cioè il can. 2195, § 1, come una vera e propria *definizione* del delitto... Se, di fatto, il vero delitto è solo quello che viene definito nel can. 2195, § 1, il caso contemplato nel can. 2222, § 1, non è un delitto...[30]

D. The General Penal Law Theory

It is the present writer's opinion that the recognition of the general penal character of canon 2222, § 1, provides the key to the harmonious and satisfactory solution of the problem. According to this interpretation, every ecclesiastical law and precept, *a priori,* is a penal norm in the exceptional case in which serious scandal or a special gravity is involved in the transgression. This solution has the advantage of preserving the integrity of the principle *nulla poena sine praevia sanctione*

28 "Nozione del Delitto," *ETL,* III (1926), 212.

29 *De Delictis et Poenis,* n. 52.

30 "Nozione del Delitto," *ETL,* III (1926), 212.

poenali and it foregoes all application of the odious principle of retroactivity in penal law. On the basis of this assumption the following article will be devoted to an integrated study of the rules of law as contained in canons 2195 and 2222, § 1.

ARTICLE III. THE GENERAL PENAL NATURE OF CANON 2222, § 1

The ordinary norm for the infliction of canonical penalties is expressed in the second part of canon 2222, § 1, where it is stated that no one can be punished unless first he has been warned with the threat of a penalty, and then has nevertheless proceeded to violate the law.[81] This is nothing more than a restatement of the principle *nulla poena sine praevia sanctione poenali,* as set forth in canon 2195.

The special faculty however which is enshrined in canon 2222, § 1, provides that under certain conditions a lawful superior is able to invoke a canonical penal sanction against the violation of a law or a precept that contains no specific threat of a penalty; and this can be done *"etiam sine praevia poenae comminatione."* As has been seen, this seeming antinomy has been explained in various ways, none of which appear to offer a consistant and satisfactory expression of the mind of the legislator.

There is another and impressive group of canonical authors[82] who regard the special penal faculty contained in canon 2222, § 1, as providing an extraordinary norm for the infliction of canonical penalties in full harmony and conformity with the principle *nulla poena sine praevia sanctione poenali.*

This interpretation argues that canon 2222, § 1, has the character of a general penal law which threatens the infliction of *"aliqua iusta poena"* in the event of certain extraordinary forms of transgression; this general but explicit threat of a

[81] Canon 2222, § 1 "...secus reus puniri nequit..."

[82] Michiels, *Normae Generales,* I, 203-205; Roberti, *De Delictis et Poenis,* n. 53; Vidal, "Notio Delicti in Iure Codicis," *Jus Pont.,* I-II (1921-1922), 101; Wernz-Vidal, *Ius Canonicum,* VII, nn. 33, 34; Beste, *Introductio In Codicem* (2. ed., Collegeville, Minn.: St. John's Abbey Press, 1944), p. 874; Noval, "De Ratione Corrigendi," *Jus. Pont.,* I-II (1921-1922), 154-155; Coronata, *Institutiones,* IV, n. 1695.

penalty suffices to induce a true delictual imputability consistent with the requirements set forth in canon 2195. From this it follows that every ecclesiastical law or precept has the nature of a penal law in the event that the scandal given or the gravity involved in the transgression is of an exceptionally serious character.[33]

It may be objected in accordance with canon 2195 that, when the lawgiver has not incorporated a specific threat of penalty in a law or a precept, its violation cannot be treated as a delict and in consequence punished with an ecclesiastical penalty.

This does not appear to be a valid objection. Neither the principle *nulla poena sine praevia sanctione poenali* nor canon 2195 requires that a specific threat of a canonical punishment be *embodied* in each individual law or precept; what is required is that a delinquent be forewarned in some way that his violation of the law or the precept invites the application of a canonical penalty. This condition is adequately fulfilled in canon 2222, § 1. For the transgressor is forewarned *by this canon* that the violation of a non-penal law or precept in which he is guilty of giving notable scandal or of perpetrating a specially grave transgression renders him subject to the infliction of some just and equitable penalty.

An attentive analysis of the terminology employed by the author of the Code supports this contention. In particular, the phrase, *"nullam sanctionem appositam,"* deserves careful consideration,[34] for it delineates the category of juridical norms within which the special faculty as granted by the canon becomes operative. The word *"appositam"* literally means: placed or situated at or near to or against; contiguous to, bordering upon.[35] As the exclusive province within which the special faculty lawfully operates, the Code designates only those juridic norms that do not *contain, incorporate,* or *embody* a canonical penalty for their violation.

[33] Canon 2222, § 1: "...si scandalum forte datum aut specialis transgressionis gravitas id ferat."

[34] Canon 2222, § 1.

[35] *Harper's Latin Dictionary* (New York: American Book Co., 1907), edited by E. A. Andrews, revised by Charlton T. Lewis and Charles Short, s.v. *appono*.

A comparison of the terminology used in this canon with that employed in canon 2195 indicates that no such incorporation of a penal threat in each individual law is required. For the words used in canon 2195— *"addita sit"* and *"adnexa sit"* —do not involve the notion of place or position, but rather the consideration of a connection or relationship; according to *Harper's Latin Dictionary,* the word *addo* is used "when a new thought is added to what precedes, as an enlargement of it, 'add to this, add to this the circumstance that'," and the word *adnecto* connotes a connection with or a binding together.[36]

From this it follows that the concept of delictual imputability simply postulates that a person be previously warned that the violation of a juridic norm will make him liable for punishment, but it is not necessary according to the prescripts of canon 2195 that the penal threat be incorporated in each individual norm. Perhaps it is with this in mind that Michiels warns:

> Imprimis sedulo notetur, quod ad punibilitatem actus canon 2195, § 1, non requirit ut norma juridica, quae violatur, sanctionem poenalem appositam habeat, sed ut ipsi violationi addita sit sanctio canonica. *Quod non est idem.*[37]

In consequence the exponents of this explanation contend that two contradictory principles are not involved in this problem, but rather that one and the same principle prevails consistently throughout the penal law of the Code. Certainly this interpretation is reflected in the canons, for canon 2222, § 1, speaks of the threat of *"aliqua iusta poena."* As has been noted, *poena* and *delictum* are employed consistently as terms of one and the same equation. The Code defines an ecclesiastical penalty as imposed only for delicts;[38] it insists that no penalty be inflicted until moral certainty is established concerning the commission of a delict.[39] The presumption prevails therefore that the canonical penalty threatened in canon 2222,

[36] Cf. *op. cit.,* s.v. *addo, adnecto.*

[37] *De Delictis et Poenis,* p. 77 (italics are inserted).

[38] Canon 2215.

[39] Canon 2233, § 1.

§1, can be imposed lawfully only in consequence of a true ecclesiastical delict, as it is defined in canon 2195.

The lack of any specific determination of the penalty threatened in canon 2222, § 1,[40] cannot be alleged as a valid objection to this solution. For canon 2195 postulates only the violation of a law to which is attached at least an indeterminate penal sanction. D'Angelo however distinguished between relative and absolute indetermination,[41] and argued that the degree of indetermination in the penal sanction as threatened in canon 2222, § 1, is so absolute that it is no longer a simple application of a duly constituted penalty, but it implies a legal enactment by a legislative superior.[42]

One may perhaps question the rightful use of the lawful superior's discretionary powers when he decides that the given scandal is of a serious character or the transgression one of a special gravity, but it is hardly convincing to accentuate the indetermination of the penal threat as contained in canon 2222, § 1, so as to place it outside the scope of the coercive power of the superior.[43]

A few of the penalties in the Code are fully determined, but the policy of the supreme lawgiver to a large extent was to authorize the inflictions of undetermined penal sanctions under well-defined conditions; but actually to determine in a given set of circumstances what constitutes a proportionate penalty is left to the prudent judgment of the local superior. A

[40] Canon 2222, § 1: "...Superior potest...aliqua iusta poena punire."

[41] "...la *determinatezza* troppo assoluta della sanzione, la quale conduce fuori ogni limite di una semplice *applicazione*."—"Nozione del Delitto," *ETL.* III (1926), 213.

[42] D'Angelo also objected to the interpretation in the sense as here proposed for the following reason: "La inutilità del dispositivo del can. 2222, § 1, quando già il can. 2220, § 1, *riconosce* nel Superiore ecclesiastico la facoltà di annettere ossia aggiungere pene a leggi e precetti."—*loc. cit.* The contemplated force of this objection is not altogether clear; the evident purpose of canon 2220, § 1, is to differentiate the enactment of canonical penalties by those who have legislative authority, and the application of them by those who are endowed with only judicial power. The substantive law of canon 2222, § 1, enunciates a general penal principle to which both legislative and judicial authority is subject.

[43] "...oportet recolere arbitrium iudicis incipere ubi cessat determinatio legis; inde potestas iudicis eo latius patet, quo minus sibi legislator adscripsit. Non est autem mirum quod amplissima potestas iudicandi de opportunitate, qualitate et quantitate poenae in hoc casu Superiori fuerit reservata."—Roberti, *De Delictis et Poenis,* n. 53.

study of the penal statutes of the Code reveals at least five gradations in the determination of penalties: 1) some penalties are completely determined, as in canons 2347, 2410; 2) a second group are determined by a maximum and a minimum, as in canons 2324, 2353, and 2385; 3) a third category merely directs that a penalty be inflicted, but remits to the superior the actual determination, as in canons 2323, 2343, and 2404; 4) another group commands the infliction of a penalty "*simpliciter pro gravitate,*" as in canons 2322, 2325, 2383, and 2386; 5) a final category of canons authorizes the superior to inflict a penalty if he prudently judges that it is necessary, and also remits to him the determination of the penalty to be inflicted; it is to this category that the indeterminate penal sanction of canon 2222, § 1, belongs, as well as several others, as contained in canons 1554, 2361 and 2391, § 2.

This policy of the Code to delegate the actual determination of the penalty to the local superior is fully justified by the fact that the local superior is in a better position to determine the nature and the measure of the penalty which is to be applied in particular cases. This policy leaves room for the better proportioned employment of equity than if all penalties were fully predetermined in the common law. Vidal (1868-1939) testified to this when he wrote:

> Quare legislatori, cuius est legem poenalem ferre, maxime congruit ut saltem obiectiva elementa delicti per conceptum a posteriori definiat, relicta iudici sola aestimatione elementorum subiectivorum quae in quolibet casu variant, cum dependeant a circumstantiis personae, quae factum delictuosum posuit. *Atque haec est illa notio in Codice tradita. . .*[44]

According to this solution, therefore, canon 2222, § 1, is a general penal law which *a priori* renders penal in character every juridic norm whose violation under extraordinary and exceptional circumstances results in scandal or gravity of transgression that is especially serious. The penal sanction contained in the canon, though it remains indeterminate in its applicable

[44] "Notio Delicti in Iure Codicis," *Jus Pont.*, I (1921), 100 (Italics are inserted).

character, supplies the juridical element postulated for delictual acts, so that the violations and transgressions in question are truly to be regarded as ecclesiastical delicts. Thus the seeming conflict between canons 2195 and 2222, § 1, is resolved, and, as Cicognani observes, the whole canon is "a verification of that juridic aphorism *"nulla poena sine lege."*[45]

Frequently the use of this special faculty as granted in canon 2222, § 1, is referred to as a "dispensation" or a "derogation" from the general law. In the light of the general penal nature of the canon it seems warranted to challenge this point of view. In other words, if the penal character of the canon supplies the juridical element which calls for such violations to be treated as true ecclesiastical delicts, from what is the superior dispensed, or in what does the law of canon 2195 suffer any derogation?

It is understood that the valid operation of the faculty granted in this canon does not depend on the acceptance of the general penal character of canon 2222, § 1, Vidal's contention to the contrary notwithstanding.[46]

The phrase "etiam sine praevia poenae comminatione"[47] does not imply a granted dispensation from the principle *nulla poena sine praevia sanctione poenali,* but the phrase serves to clarify the lawful use of the faculty under the conditions set forth in the canon. It removes from the realm of theory and opinion the authority granted in the canon, and permits the infliction of penalties whenever the lawful superior prudently judges that the scandal given or the gravity of transgression is especially serious. Therefore no true dispensation or derogation is involved.

Nonetheless, there is a dispensation or derogation in a limited sense. The ordinary norm for the infliction of canonical penalties requires that the law or the precept contain a specific penal threat, and usually the violation of laws and precepts that do not embody a definite penal warning cannot be punished as true delicts. However, when the conditions of canon 2222,

[45] *Canon Law,* p. 507.

[46] "Notio Delicti in Iure Codicis," *Jus Pont.,* I (1921), 101.

[47] Canon 2222, § 1.

§ 1, are verified, a derogation or a dispensation from this ordinary norm is provided so that such violations which involve a specially serious scandal or evince an unusual gravity can be treated as true ecclesiastical delicts.

It is true that this interpretation accords to the principle *nulla poena sine praevia sanctione poenali* a liberal construction in contrast to the strict interpretation that the principle receives, at least in theory, in the penal codes of the secular law. But, as has been noted, even in the secular law it has been found necessary at times in the interests of the common good to circumvent the severity of this principle with the use of general penal laws.[48] The lawgiver of the Code has recognized this need, and through canon 2222, § 1, has provided a legal safeguard in the interests of the common good of society against the possible harm that could, and at times certainly would, result from a rigid and absolute application of the principle which denies the applicability of all penalties in the absence of a penal law.

[48] Seagle, *The Quest for Law*, p. 247.

CHAPTER SIX

LAWFUL USE OF THE EXTRAORDINARY PENAL FACULTY

ARTICLE I.

JURIDIC SCOPE OF THE EXTRAORDINARY FACULTY

It is important to remember that no matter what theoretical solution is accepted for the purpose of inducing harmony between the norms enunciated in canons 2222, § 1, and 2195, it in no way interferes with the lawful exercise of the special authority granted by the Code to competent superiors. It is the theory which correctly explains the special faculty, and not the faculty itself, that is subject to controversy.

Vidal, so it appears, fell into this error when he stated:

> Atque etiam praescindendo a charactere poenali illius canonis, potius in eo firmatur quod, extra casum praeviae legis aut praecepti poenalis, legis transgressio imputari ad poenam non potest, nisi praecesserit monitio cum comminatione poenae. . .illa quoque exceptio de speciali scandalo aut speciali transgressionis gravitate pariter in idem principium generale recedit.[1]

Any assertion that renders the valid operation of the authority granted in canon 2222, § 1, dependent on the recognition of some particular explanation is entirely unacceptable.[2]

The various opinions that have been projected for the purpose of harmonizing the law as enacted in canons 2195 and 2222, § 1, were discussed in the preceding chapter; it is noteworthy that not one of these interpretations questions the fact

[1] "Notio Delicti in Iure Codicis," *Jus Pont.*, I (1921), 101

[2] "Grave scandalum, gravissimi iuris laesio, in se continent publici boni perturbationem, cui castigandae praecedat necesse est Superioris praeceptum quo transgressor adigatur cum comminatione poenae. . ."—Vidal, *loc. cit.*

that a valid grant of authority has been made by the lawgiver.[3] One can agree that, unless the general penal character of this canon is recognized, it is difficult to offer a consistent and harmonious expression of the mind of the legislator of the Code; but the ultimate right of lawful superiors in virtue of canon 2222, § 1, to impose a proportionate penalty *"etiam sine praevia poenae comminatione"* is in no way contingent on the acceptance of any one theoretical interpretation.

On the other hand, Cammeo appears to have misinterpreted the faculty which is made available through canon 2222, § 1. In comparing the penal authority as granted in this canon with Article 23 of the Constitution for the Vatican State,[4] he asserts the need of a special warning before the infliction of a penalty, for he says: "Le differenze fra il can. 2222, § 1, e l'articolo qui esaminato sono molteplici: . . .nel canone il Superiore interviene con un' ammonizione comminatoria che ha carattere di *lex specialis,* e la pena si applica alle trasgressioni successive: nell'art. 23 il giudice, se lo crede giusto, punisce senz'altro."[5]

For irregardless of the theory that correctly interprets the canon, the lawful superior is authorized to inflict a penalty without any previous warning whenever the essential conditions are verified in fact.

The vast range of ecclesiastical legislation which is subject to the general penal norm of canon 2222, § 1, reflects the overall importance of this extraordinary faculty.[6] A relatively

[3] ". . .certum est, ex can. 2222, § 1, quod ad scandalum speciale vel specialiter gravem legis transgressionem punienda poena quadem vindicativa, nulla requiritur praevia monitio cum comminatione poenae."—Michiels, *Normae Generales,* I, 204.

[4] Art. 23, n. 11: "Si forte normae poenales legislationis regni Italici, ut suppletoriae admissae, quamcumque ob causam applicari non possint, neque alia peculiaris poenalis dispositio praestet, et tamen aliquid fuerit admissum quod religionem et bonos mores, ordinem publicum et personarum rerumve securitatem offendat, iudex, salvis cautionibus et poenis spiritualibus Iuris Canonici, potest delinquentem punire, vel mulcta ad 9000 libellarum, vel carcere ad sex menses."; cf. F. Cammeo, *Ordinamento Giuridico dello Stato della Citta del Vaticano* (Firenze: Bemporad, 1932) p. 238.

[5] Cammeo, *Ordinamento Giuridico dello Stato della Citta del Vaticano,* p. 228.

[6] Michiels, *De Delictis et Poenis,* pp. 81, 82. Among the many violations that are punishable in virtue of this special faculty of canon 2222, § 1, this author mentions: ". . .fornicatio a clerico admissa (can. 132, § 1). . ."—*Loc. cit.* However, it seems that the Code has made adequate provision regarding the punishment of this delict in canons 2358 and 2359, § 3.

small minority of juridic norms contain an express penal clause.[7] This fact does not imply that the common lawgiver failed to foresee that in certain exceptional cases the violation of the non-penal juridic norms would seriously disrupt the social order, nor does it mean that such transgressions are to pass with impunity:[8] rather, it confirms the reason for the canonical provision in canon 2222, § 1, in the light of which such exceptional violations can be treated as true ecclesiastical delicts according to the needs of each individual case.[9]

The juridic boundaries within which the special authority granted in canon 2222, § 1, is intended to operate are not immediately apparent from a cursory reading of the canon, which says only: *"Licet lex nullam sanctionem appositam habeat. . ."* From this it is understood that the violation pertains only to a law which a person is legally obliged to observe, but which is enacted without a sanction that carries a specific penal threat. Therefore if scandal emerges entirely apart from the violation of a law or precept or if the juridic norm contains a penal clause, the special authority which is granted in this canon finds no lawful application.

The applicability of this special faculty with reference to violations of the divine law, of the common law of the Code, and of particular legislation will each be given a separate consideration.

A. The Divine Law

Canonical writers are not in agreement among themselves concerning the lawful use of the special penal authority that has been enacted in canon 2222, § 1, to punish violations solely of the divine law. The foundation of all ecclesiastical law is the natural or positive divine law but there are many prescripts of the divine law that do not also form a part of the positive ecclesiastical law. It is in regard to this latter category that

7 The Code of Canon Law consists of 2414 canons; of these, only 101 embody the threat of penalty.

8 Wernz-Vidal, *Ius Canonicum,* VII, n. 34.

9 "Iam nunc nulla violatio legis universalis vi iuris communis aliqua poena puniri potest, nisi quando et quia et quatenus in Codice J. C. poena determinata vel indeterminata sit ipsi adnexa, *servato sane can. 2222."*— Michiels, *De Delictis et Poenis,* p. 40.

the problem arises concerning the lawful application of the special faculty granted in canon 2222, § 1.

In the general abrogation of all universal laws that are not contained in the common law of the Code, an explicit exception was made relative to the divine law.[10] However this exception should be understood in the sense that it calls attention to the fact that it is beyond the power and authority of every human lawgiver to abrogate in any way the prescripts of the divine law. It is the opinion of the present writer that the scope of the special penal power granted in canon 2222, § 1, is limited to violations of *positive ecclesiastical law* and that it does not find lawful application in regard to transgressions of the positive or natural divine law unless at the same time some juridic norm of ecclesiastical legislation has been violated.[11]

Canon 2222, § 1, itself requires only the violation of a non-penal *law*[12] but this interpretation that restricts the scope of its penal authority is preferable in view of the basic assumption that the principles and prescripts contained in the Code are applicable only to positive ecclesiastical legislation.[13]

There is no doubt that any act or omission contrary to the divine law brings moral guilt, but the presence of such guilt does not necessarily imply also the presence of *delictual* guilt which alone warrants the infliction of penal sanctions. Relative to this doctrine, Wernz-Vidal taught:

> Transgressio intelligitur legis *ecclesiasticae* (cui ab Ecclesia addita sit sanctio): . . .transgressio legis naturalis et divinae non dicit relationem ad magisterium poenale potestatis publicae quae societati praeest, nisi in quantum ab hac, quod naturali et divino iure edicitur, praescribatur

10 Canon 6, 6°.

11 "Iam vero in casu nostro lex adest. Non enim potest Superior poenam irrogare pro actu malo qui iam non exstet aliqua lege positiva prohibitus . . .atque in hoc stat progressus novi Codicis."—Roberti, *De Delictis et Poenis*, n. 53.

12 "Licet lex nullam sanctionem appositam habeat. . ."

13 ". . .in Codice poenali certae dumtaxat iuris naturalis transgressiones puniuntur. Quare in violatione legis divinae, si praescindatur a lege ecclesiastica, habetur actus illicitus et peccatum, cui ratio delicti et punibilitas in foro externo et sociali accedit ex prohibitione et sanctione canonica." —Wernz-Vidal, *Ius Canonicum*, VII, n. 29.

> aut prohibeatur, sine qua lege iuris naturalis transgressio, quae hominem etiam extra societatem ligat, dicet respectum ad ordinem *moralem generalem* et erit *peccatum* divinae sanctioni obnoxium, *non delictum.*[14]

Hence it follows that punishment for violations of the purely divine law are left to divine judgment and the principle prevails that only the violation of an ecclesiastical law constitutes a delict and is the exclusive object of an ecclesiastical penalty.[15]

This restrictive interpretation receives support from the canonical provision for supplementary legislation enacted in canon 20. In this canon, the lawgiver directs that when the application of penalties is involved, the authority granted is in no way applicable.[16] Consonant with the principle *nulla poena sine lege,* the lawful use of a canonical penalty requires an express penal clause in the law or precept.

Again in canon 2221 this interpretation that restricts the scope of canon 2222, § 1, appears to be implied. For the former canon provides for the lawful enactment of penalties in the matter of especially serious violations of the divine law; the absence of a similar provision in canon 2222, § 1, argues for the opinion that the penal authority therein granted is not available unless a violation of some positive ecclesiastical norm is involved.[17]

In reference to this problem, Sole (+ 1921) favored the non-applicability of the norm enacted in canon 2222, § 1, when the violation did not involve an ecclesiastical law:

> Hic legem poenalem non accipimus legem divinam sive positivam sive naturalem, cuius violatio peccatum facit et non delictum, sed humanum tantum... si lex divina sive

14 *Ius Canonicum,* VII, n. 29.

15 Michiels, *De Delictis et Poenis,* p. 62.

16 Canon 20. Si certa de re desit expressum praescriptum legis sive generalis sive particularis, norma sumenda est, *nisi agatur de poenis applicandis...* (Italics are inserted).

17 ...ob peculiaria rerum adiuncta, legem tam divinam, quam ecclesiasticam a superiore potestate latam, in territorio vigentem, congrua poena munire aut poenam lege statutam aggravare."—Canon 2221.

positiva sive naturalis, etiam a lege ecclesiastica muniatur aliqua poena, tunc conditur ius humanum positivum poenale eiusque violatio, externa et moraliter imputabilis, delictum constituit.[18]

Both Michiels and Berutti adopted this view that only the violation of an *ecclesiastical* law or precept justified the infliction of a canonical penalty.[19]

Noval (1861-1938) and Coronata subscribed to the contrary view in this difficulty when they acknowledged the authority granted in canon 2222, § 1, as applicable also in the event of violations of the divine law even though it did not involve the violation of an ecclesiastical law or precept.[20]

It is true that this opposite opinion possessses probability on its side, and for that reason can be accepted. But the present writer believes that the more restrictive opinion is the preferable one. Penal legislation is subject to a strict interpretation,[21] and in cases where doubt is established concerning the extension of a penal norm, the less extensive interpretation should be followed.[22] Therefore the assumption is warranted that the legislator of the Code of Canon Law restricted the application of the penal norms to transgressions of ecclesiastical law, and hence the juridic scope of the special penal faculty as granted in canon 2222, § 1, is limited to violations of positive ecclesiastical law or precept.

B. The Common Law of the Code

It is evident that the special faculty as contained in canon 2222, § 1, provides authority for punishing the violation of

18 *De Delictis et Poenis,* n. 6; cf. also ibid., n. 85.

19 "Iam vero vi principii in can. 2222, § 1, enuntiati, *omnis lex ecclesiastica... censenda est poenalis.*"—Michiels, *De Delictis et Poenis,* p. 80; cf. also Berutti, *Institutiones Iuris Canonici* (5 vols., Romae: Marietti, 1936-1943), VI, 75.

20 "...legislator suo praescripto canonis 2222, § 1, tribuit Superiori facultatem infligendi poenam ab ipso determinatam pro transgressione cuiuslibet legis etiam mere naturalis..."—"De Ratione Corrigendi," *Jus Pont.,* I-II (1921-1922), 155; Coronata, *Pene e Sanzioni Canoniche Estragiudiziali* (Torino: L.I.C.E.—Berutti, 1933), n. 21.

21 Canon 19.

22 Canons 15 and 2119, § 1.

any non-penal canon of the Code whenever the violation has resulted in notable scandal or evinces a special gravity. For the most part the canons which embody a penal clause are designed for the protection of society from common dangers. When a prescript of the common law contains a specific penal threat, this fact reflects the judgment of the legislator that its violation represents a threat to society in view of the gravity of the law or because of the danger of a frequent violation.

Among the laws of the Code that contain no specific threat of punishment by way of penal sanction are the canons that relate to the reading of forbidden books that have not been prohibited by name in some papal document,[23] to the obligation of annual confession and communion,[24] and to many of the canons that regulate the life of the clergy, especially in secular affairs.[25] In the absence of some specific penal legislation, the violation of these canons ordinarily cannot be punished as a delict; but if such a violation involves notable scandal or particular seriousness, the special faculty as granted in canon 2222, § 1, authorizes the superior to treat it as a true ecclesiastical delict.

The practical function of this special faculty can be illustrated in connection with the common law legislation that requires clerics to abstain from all things that are unbecoming to their state.[26] Relative to this the Code establishes definite juridic obligations to avoid all secular activities that are foreign to the priestly vocation, to forego hunting especially with display and publicity, to refrain from visiting saloons apart from necessity or without a just cause approved by the ordinary. However, the legislator did not impose these obligations under threat of any specific penalty. Nonetheless, a violation that results in notable scandal or special gravity can be punished with a proportionate penalty imposed in virtue of the special authority which canon 2222, § 1, grants to the competent superior.[27]

23 Cf. Canon 1399.

24 Cf. Canons 859, 906.

25 Cf. Canons 124-144.

26 Canon 138.

27 "Missionarius vero e clero saeculari vel regulari, qui Orientalem quempiam ad latinam ritum consilio auxiliove inducat, vi can. 2222, § 1, puniri potest." —Petrani, "De S. C. pro Ecclesia Orientali," *Apollinaris,* X (1937), 39.

Similarly, the Code provides penal legislation with reference to apostates and fugitives from religious communities.[28] But Beste points out[29] that a religious with temporary vows who is guilty of an unlawful departure with the intention of not returning cannot be classified in either category and thus escapes the common law penalties. Yet, although he is neither an apostate nor a fugitive in the strict sense of canon 644, his action becomes punishable in consequence of the faculty enacted in canon 2222, § 1, even with dismissal from the religious life, in accordance with canon 647.

The usefulness of this faculty in the protection of the sanctity of marriage is suggested by the Sacred Congregation of the Sacraments in its instruction concerning pre-nuptial investigations.[30] This instruction directs ordinaries to enforce its rulings by using, if it should prove necessary, the authority granted in canon 2222, § 1.[31] The Code has enacted severe penalties for those who attempt marriage while still held by a prior and still-existing bond;[32] however, no specific penalties are established for those who are guilty of simulating consent and who bring public ridicule upon the sacrament with pacts and intentions that make a mockery of the sacred union. Bartoccetti suggests that in such cases ordinaries use the special faculty granted them in canon 2222, § 1, by inflicting canonical penalties in reparation for the harm done.[33]

28 Canons 644; 645; 2385; 2386.

29 *Introductio in Codicem,* pp. 436-437.

30 29 iun. 1941, n. 12—*AAS,* (1949) XXXIII, 306-307.

31 "Haec Sacra Congregatio, gravissima incommoda quae ex illicitis atque irritis nuptiis eveniunt prae oculis habens, locorum Ordinarios deprecatur ut, pro sua pastorali sollicitudine, cum parochis traditas cautelas communicent omnique cura advigilent ut exsecutioni mandentur, canonicasque poenas infligere ne omittant in negligentes ad normam can. 2222, § 1, haud exclusa suspensione a divinis, praesertim in recidivos, quo tutius nuptiarum rectae celebrationi prospiciatur, cuiusvis offensionis periculo remoto, prout sacramenti matrimonii dignitatem et sanctitatem decet."—*Loc. cit.*

32 Canon 2356.

33 "In casu autem nostro, celebratio matrimonii cum pacto vel cum intentione excludendi indissolubilitatem vel bonum prolis aut fidei certo certius est talis transgressio quae ex se sola sufficeret ut Ordinarius e suo tribunali eiiceret tales culpabiles coniuges suam turpitudinem ostentantes..."—"De Iure et Officio Promotoris Iustitiae Accusandi Matrimonium," *Apollinaris,* X (1937), 582.

From these few illustrations one can note the practical consequences of the special faculty granted in canon 2222, § 1. It has been remarked that a large majority of the canons do not contain a penal clause, and that ordinarily the violation of these non-penal canons does not subject the guilty person to the use of punitive measures against him. But whenever the superior discerns a notable scandal or a special gravity in connection with the violation of a non-penal law, the authority as granted in this canon allows him in the interests of common good to impose a proportionate penalty upon the guilty subject.

C. Particular Legislation

The penal principles of the common law apply with equal vigor to the legislation passed by subordinate legislators for their jurisdictions. According to the axiom, "*Ubi lex non distinguit, nec nos distinguere debemus,*" the special faculty vindicated in canon 2222, § 1, is validly applicable to the legislative enactments of local ordinaries, as well as to the statutes enacted in diocesan synods and to the decrees issued in provincial councils.

Moreover, the Code expressly states: "*quae dicuntur de delictis, applicantur etiam violationibus praecepti*";[34] consequently all jurisdictional precepts[35] issued by competent superiors, although not accompanied with any specific threat of a penalty are amenable to the special faculty granted in canon 2222, § 1, in the event of notable scandal or of a specially grave transgression.[36]

The lawful use of this extraordinary authority against strangers (*peregrini*) is in need of clarification. Canon 14 establishes the general rule that persons outside their proper territory are not bound to observe either the particular laws of their own territory or the particular laws of the territory in which they are staying. However, there are exceptions to this general law: the particular laws of one's own territory must be observed if the violation of them would prove harm-

[34] Canon 2195, § 2.

[35] Canons 24 and 2225.

[36] Noval, "De Ratione Corrigendi," *Jus Pont.*, I-II (1921-1922), 155; Michiels, *De Delictis et Poenis*, p. 80.

ful to that territory or if the law is personal in character; the particular laws of the territory in which the stranger temporarily resides must be observed by him only if they concern the public order or the formalities required for acts and contracts.[37]

It is entirely outside the scope of this article to enter the controversial discussion concerning the laws which pertain to the public order or which if violated prove harmful to a person's proper territory.[38] For the purpose of this study it will suffice to point out that canon 2222, § 1, does not create juridic obligations; rather, the special faculty as vindicated in this canon is lawfully exercised only in relation to violations of the laws and precepts which bound the stranger by a prior juridic obligation, and when the non-observance was accompanied with a serious scandal or a special gravity in the guilt.

All authors are agreed that strangers are bound to observe the particular laws of a territory when the non-observance would cause scandal in the proper sense of the word.[39] This is a moral obligation founded in the natural law; not all, however, are agreed that this is also a juridic obligation; and the special faculty as granted in canon 2222, § 1, seems to become applicable only upon the violation of juridic obligations.

Van Hove (1872-1947) stated that in virtue of canon 2222, § 1, the ordinary can inflict a penalty for every transgression of law in the case of scandal.[40] Without entering the dispute as to whether a juridic obligation to avoid the occasioning of scandal arises from canon 14, the present writer believes that canon 2222, § 1, is not the source of that obligation. For this canon presupposes an already existing juridic obligation.

37 Canon 14, 1° and 2°.

38 "Dici fortasse possit, *ordini publico* consuli per eas leges quae ad commune damnum avertendum potius quam ad promovendum bonum commune latae sunt."—Vermeersch-Creusen, *Epitome,* I, n. 110; Wernz-Vidal, *Ius Canonicum,* I, n. 156; Michiels, *Normae Generales,* I, 318.

39 Wernz-Vidal, *Ius Canonicum,* I, n. 156; Van Hove, "Leges Quae Ordini Publico Consulunt,"*ETL,* I (1924), 161; Michiels, *Normae Generales,* I, 320; Cicognani, *Canon Law,* p. 581.

40 "En vertu du canon 2222, § 1, ordinarire peut, en cas de scandale, infliger une peine pour toute transgression d'une loi, même si le droit n'en a prévu aucune."—"Leges Quae Ordini Publico Consulunt," *ETL,* I (1924), 160.

Van Hove spoke here of penalties inflicted in virtue of canon 2222, § 1, for violations of law to which a person was held not by reason of the law, but solely in view of the emergence of scandal.[41] It seems that his interpretation accords to the special faculty as granted in canon 2222, § 1, an unwarranted extension, so that scandal could be punished whenever and wherever found, apart from any relation to a preexisting juridic obligation.

The opinion is here expressed that this canon was not enacted for this extensive purpose. A true juridic obligation to observe a law is not simply presumed but rather that obligation is binding only upon proof of its existence. In cases where the obligation of observing a law is doubtful, the lawgiver has resolved that doubt in favor of the freedom of the subject.[42] The lawful exercise of the special authority granted in canon 2222, § 1, postulates a violation of a non-penal law or precept which the transgressor was bound to observe by a true juridic obligation. It is true that the legislator speaks of scandal in this canon, but this element is not the direct object of the penal power that is granted, but rather scandal is the *conditio sine qua non;* when the lawful superior finds that this essential condition is fulfilled and that this element of scandal intensifies the guilt imputable to the transgressor of a non-penal law or precept, the special penal authority of this canon becomes operative. The more liberal interpretation that allows the use of this extraordinary faculty for the inflicting of canonical penalties against those who have occasioned scandal entirely apart from any violation of a juridic obligation does not seem to be justified in the light of the prescript of canon 2222, § 1.

The use of the special faculty as contained in canon 2222, § 1, involves not only the application of a *penal norm* but also an *exception* to the ordinary penal norm; as such, it is subject to a strict interpretation.[43] The opinion that the special author-

41 "Si l'etranger est tenu... de la loi qu'à raison du scandale, cette peine ne lui sera pas applicable, puisqu'il n'est pas soumis à la loi; toutefois l'Ordinaire pourra lui infliger une peine proportionée à la faute."—"Leges Quae Ordini Publico Consulunt," *ETL,* (1934), 161.

42 Canon 15: Leges, etiam irritantes et inhabilitantes, in dubio iuris non urgent.

43 Canons 19 and 2219, § 1.

ity granted in this canon may be directed against scandal without regard to any definite and prior juridic obligation for the observance of the law in question does not seem to conform to this basic rule of penal interpretation.

A circular letter of the Sacred Congregation of the Council in 1926 directed the attention of ordinaries to the conduct of priests visiting outside their proper dioceses for reasons of health or recreation.[44] This document is interpreted by some as implying authorization for the use of the special faculty mentioned in canon 2222, § 1, with a view to punishing the scandalous conduct of visiting clergy without regard to preexisting laws to which strangers are held.[45] This interpretation seems definitely unwarranted, for the letter of the Sacred Congregation directed the *enactment* of suitable penal laws which the *sacerdos peregrinus* would be bound to observe.[46] This letter in directing the enactment of suitable penal laws for the punishment of scandalous conduct would indeed have called for something superfluous if the special faculty as vindicated in canon 2222, § 1, could be as extensively interpreted as Van Hove and some other authors have suggested. The promulgation of penal laws for strangers establishes definite juridic obligations, and thereby renders unnecessary any and all recourse to the special faculty granted in canon 2222, § 1.

In this regard it is the competent superior, and not the individual stranger, who must determine which particular territorial laws pertain to the public order and thus become binding for visitors who come into the territory.[47] In the event that the ordinary binds strangers to the observance of definite particular laws that do not contain penal threats, the violation of any of these laws under the accompaniment of notable scandal or of a special gravity in the transgression could be punished in virtue of the special faculty granted in canon 2222, § 1.

[44] 1 iul. 1926, n. 6—*AAS* XVIII (1926), 312.

[45] Bouscaren, *Canon Law Digest,* I, 845.

[46] N. 6: "Ut autem hi sacerdotes facilius in officio contineantur, (Ordinarii) opportunas poenas constituant quibus officientur si scandalum dederint, vel si quoquo modo aliquid egerint, quod sacerdotali munere indignum sit."—*AAS,* XVIII (1926), 313.

[47] "Nimis enim evidens est exceptionem non ita intelligi debere quod ipsius peregrini seu advenae iudicio relinquatur..."—Wernz-Vidal, *Ius Canonicum,* I, n. 156.

ARTICLE II. NOTABLE SCANDAL AND SPECIAL GRAVITY

The essential condition[48] upon which depends the valid exercise of the special authority granted in canon 2222, § 1, is the element of notable scandal or of an exceptional gravity in the transgression. This is a *conditio sine qua non,* for in the absence of scandal that is more serious than the scandal that ordinarily arises from a public delict or unless the gravity of the violation is aggravated by some added factor or circumstance, the lawgiver withholds this special authority which warrants the inflicting of a canonical penalty without a previous warning.[49] The fact that the lawful use of this special faculty is contingent on the presence of notable scandal or of a special gravity in the transgression is indicated by the use of the particle *"si."*[50]

It should be noted that scandal is understood in this canon in its strict sense as defined below. It may be true that sometimes canonical scandal is interpreted in its wider connotation to include wonderment and astonishment that would lead to harmful misunderstanding of ecclesiastical action. Scandal in this wider sense could occasion the withholding of a benefit or a favor, such as a dispensation from a marriage impediment. But canon 2222, § 1, exists as a penal norm; it bestows extraordinary authority for the inflicting of canonical penalties in consequence of ecclesiastical delicts; as such it is subject to a strict interpretation.[51]

It is true that in the canon itself there is not to be found any express requirement that the degree of the scandal be more intensive than that of ordinary scandal. Nonetheless, a study of the canon in its text and context reveals that the special authorization to inflict a canonical penalty without a specific

48 Canon 2222, § 1: "...si scandalum forte datum aut specialis transgressionis gravitas id ferat..."

49 "Si scandalum est illud ordinarium, maius vel minus, quod quamlibet transgressionem gravem et publicam consequitur, et gravitas transgressionis non aggravatur aliqua peculiari circumstantia, legislator non confert Superiori facultatem infligendi absque monitione et comminatione aliquam poenam, nec in iudicio nec extra."—Noval, De Ratione Corrigendi," *Jus Pont.,* I-II (1921-1922), 39.

50 Canon 39.

51 Canon 19.

warning is not operative when only ordinary scandal is involved.[52]

This requirement is implicit in the fact that every grave and public violation of law results in ordinary scandal. It must be assumed that the lawgiver foresaw this fact, and nonetheless promulgated a body of law in which the majority of the canons do not contain specific warnings of penalties. The infliction of penalties for the violation of non-penal laws when the scandal is in no way exceptional would be tantamount to a correctional attitude towards the lawgiver, and to the unwarranted assumption that a defective legislation needs correction on a wholesale basis.

A study of parallel canons supports this interpretation.[53] Under the Title *"De Superiore potestatem coactivam habente,"* canon 2221 authorizes subordinate superiors to enact a new penalty or to intensify an existing penalty for a law promulgated by a superior legislative authority, but only *"ob peculiaria rerum adiuncta"*; likewise, in canon 2223, § 1, when an ecclesiastical judge inflicts a penalty already determined by law, the penalty can not be increased *"nisi extraordinaria adiuncta aggravantia id exigant."*

Scandal is defined as any word or deed, evil in itself or having the appearance of evil, that offers the occasion of sin to others. Scandal is divided into active and passive, depending on whether one advert to the scandalizing agent or the scandalized victim; again, it is direct or indirect, depending on whether it is both foreseen and intended or merely foreseen. Passive scandal is subdivided into *"scandalum datum et scandalum acceptum."*[54]

The phrase *"scandalum forte datum"* is employed in canon 2222, § 1. This fact as well as the nature of the canon imply

[52] Noval, *loc. cit.*: "Dico, notabiliter et indubie scandalosae. . ."; Berutti, *Institutiones Iuris Canonici,* VI, 75; Vidal, "Notio Delicti in Iure Codicis," *Jus Pont.,* (1921), 101

[53] Canon 18. Leges ecclesiasticae intelligendae sunt secundum propriam verborum significationem in textu et contextu consideratam; quae si dubia et obscura manserit, ad locos Codicis parallelos, si qui sint, ad legis finem ac circumstantias et ad mentem legislatoris est recurrendum.

[54] S. Thomas Aquinas, *Summa Theologica,* (6 vols., Taurini: Marietti, 1932), IIa, IIae, qu, 43, art. 1; Aertnys-Damen, *Theologia Moralis* (14. ed., 2 vols., Taurinorum Augustae: Marietti, 1944), I, nn. 376-386; Merkelbach, *Summa Theologiae Moralis* (3. ed., 3 vols., Parisiis: Desclee, 1939), I, n. 958.

that only scandal in its strict sense justifies the use of the special penal faculty. For the words "scandal given" signify an act, that, by its very nature, presents the temptation or occasion of sin to another. If the sin of the one scandalized can be imputed to his own malice, ignorance or weakness, it is a *scandalum acceptum* and does not suffice to fulfill the condition on which is postulated the use of the faculty which canon 2222, § 1, grants to the lawful superior.[55] It is irrelevant whether or not the sin of another actually was committed; it is essential and sufficient only that the nature of the act and the circumstances under which it took place are such as to induce sin in another.[56] This fact is emphasized by the insertion of the word "forte" in modification of the word "datum."

It is clear, then, that the special faculty enshrined in canon 2222, § 1, becomes validly operative only when scandal in its strict sense is given, and when it is more than ordinarily serious. By way of illustration, one may delineate the case in which a cleric has violated the canons which prohibit the visitation of public taverns, shows or theaters.[57] His violation of these canons may in fact have resulted in scandal, which however was no more grave than the lawgiver presumably foresaw. In the absence of particular legislation, no penalty can be lawfully inflicted.[58] If however the scandal was intensified by some such aggravating circumstances as the frequency of the visits, the company of the delinquent, or the nature of his conduct, the offense could be adjudged as delictual, and accordingly a canonical penalty could be inflicted apart from all warning other than that already contained in canon 2222, § 1.

The *special* gravity of the transgression is not easily defined; no ecclesiastical penalty can be inflicted at any time unless the violation of the law is imputable as a mortal sin.[59] Usually, in this case, some circumstantial factor of time, place or rank of the person guilty of a transgression which is in itself grave

55 Noldin-Schmitt, *Summa Theologiae Moralis* (24. ed., 3 vols., Romae: Pustet, 1936), II, nn. 102, 105.

56 Merkelbach, *op. cit.*, I, n. 964.

57 Canons 138 and 140.

58 Canon 2222, § 1: "...secus reus punire nequit..."

59 Canon 2218, § 2.

will aggravate the seriousness and verify the postulated condition. Coronata suggests that the *habitual* disregard of a non-penal law or a manifest display of contempt and impudence on the part of the delinquent would suffice to justify the infliction of a proportionate penalty according to the norms of canon 2222, § 1.[60] A pastor therefore who habitually ignored the canonical prescripts concerning the publication of the banns before marriage[61] could be punished by his bishop in virtue of the extraordinary faculty granted in this canon. In fact, the Sacred Congregation of the Sacraments directs ordinaries to invoke the authority of canon 2222, § 1, *"praesertim in recidivos,"* when necessary, in order to enforce the Instruction of 1941 concerning pre-nuptial investigations.[62]

Very frequently, in practice, the two conditions of notable scandal and of a special gravity of a transgression will co-exist in a violation of law, but it is evident that this is not necessary before the special faculty can rightfully be used by the superior.[63] A violation of law can be exceptionally serious apart from the element of scandal in any form; it is equally true that a transgression of a non-penal law can become amenable to coercive measures by reason exclusively of some notable scandal that has resulted.[64]

The final determination of the presence of this essential condition rests in the prudent judgment of the ecclesiastical superior. There is no mathematically objective standard by which notable scandal or exceptional gravity can be measured. The moral certainty that the scandal or the gravity is of an extraordinary character will be gained from a careful consideration of the varying factors of circumstance that surround

60 "Casus specialis gravitatis esset si legis non poenalis transgressio fieret cum gravi communitatis perturbatione; aut cum magna delinquentis impudentia ut, e.g., si delinquens delicto commisso de hac re gloriaretur; vel transgressio fieret a Superiore cui onus incumbit legis observantiam curandi."—*Manuale Practicum Iuris Disciplinaris et Criminalis Regularium* (Romae: Marietti, 1938), n. 21 (hereafter cited *Manuale Practicum*); cf. also, *Institutiones,* IV, n .1695.

61 Canons 1022-1024.

62 29 iun. 1941, n. 12—*AAS,* XXXIII (1941), 306-307.

63 "...scandalum forte datum *aut* specialis transgressionis gravitas..."

64 Coronata, *Institutiones,* n. 1695.

the violation,[65] together with the general canonical principles established by the supreme legislator. Of prime importance in the formation of this judgment is the nature of canon 2222, § 1, which constitutes an exceptional penal norm,[66] and therefore remains subject to a strict interpretation.[67] If doubts of law or fact emerge from this consideration concerning the presence of the essential condition for the valid use of this extraordinary faculty,[68] the person in question gains the favor of the law. For as Cocchi points out, it is better that a delict go unpunished than that a penalty be imposed on an innocent party.[69]

Relative to this point Vidal stated that a presumption in favor of ecclesiastical superiors exists when a doubt arises concerning the valid exercise of their public authority; however, he asserts that the contrary presumption prevails in the exercise of coercive power:

> At potestas unius hominis in alterum, quae sese extendat ad ipsum puniendum eumque privandum etiam iuribus ex ipsa natura sibi cohaerentibus, tam exorbitans apparet potestas quae debeat niti clarissima lege, non notione aliqua abstracta, quae disputationibus et controversiis sit obnoxia. Unde facile apparet praesumptionem contrariam in tantae potestatis exercitio praevalere debere: nemo me potest punire atque legitimis iuribus spoliare, nisi potestatem illam indubitabili ratione demonstret.[70]

It follows as a corollary that the special authority as vindicated in canon 2222, § 1, is not intended to be used as a normal

65 Canon 2228. Poena lege statuta non incurritur, nisi delictum fuerit in suo genere perfectum secundum proprietatem verborum legis.

66 Canon 2222, § 1: "...secus reus punire nequit nisi prius monitus..."

67 Canon 19.

68 Canon 15; 2228; 2233, § 1.

69 "...manente dubio favendum est reo; hinc, in dubio facti, aut in dubio an Titius *sit auctor facti,* nemo damanndus est, et satius est impunitum relinqui facinus nocentis, quam innocentem condemnari."—*Commentarium in Codicem Iuris Canonici ad Usum Scholarum* (8 vols. in 5, Vol. VIII, 4. ed., Taurinorum Augustae: Casa Editrice Marietti, 1938), VIII, n. 48.

70 "Notio Delicti in Iure Codicis," *Jus Pont.,* I (1921), 99.

canonical procedure; its use is constituted as an exceptional form of coercive action, and therefore its use in inflicting ecclesiastical sanctions is of an extraordinary character.[71] On the other hand, the extraordinary nature of this authority does not interfere with its lawful use when, in the prudent judgment of the competent ecclesiastical superior, the requisite conditions set forth in the canon are verified in individual cases.

71 "Usus autem huius potestatis natura rei extraordinarius manebit."—Vermeersch-Creusen, *Epitome,* III, n. 383; Chelodi-Ciprotti, *De Delictis et Poenis,* nn. 2, 25; D'Angelo, "Nozione del Delitto," *ETL,* III (1926), 217; Salucci, *Il Diritto Penale,* I, 106.

CHAPTER SEVEN

CANONICAL PROCEDURE

INTRODUCTION

A study of the special faculty granted in canon 2222, § 1, is not primarily an investigation in canonical procedure. This is not to say that there are no procedural problems in the employment of its penal authority; for, as shall be seen, the practical application of this extraordinary penal faculty involves various questions that do not yield to easy solution. The fact remains however that canon 2222, § 1, is a penal norm designed for the punishment of true ecclesiastical delicts according to the usual canonical processes provided by the Code in Book Four.

Foremost among these problems is the need to determine the nature of the jurisdiction required for the inflicting of a canonical penalty in virtue of this canon. A solution to this problem is essential to a consideration of the scope of the term *legitimus superior* who has been designated as the recipient of this special authority; it also involves the nature of process that is required for the application of the penal sanction.

ARTICLE I. THE LAWFUL SUPERIOR

Ecclesiastical jurisdiction may be defined as the public power to rule the faithful in the interests of the common good with a view to their eternal salvation.[1] By reason of the forum in which it is exercised, the power of jurisdiction is designated as being of the internal or the external forum.[2] Complete ecclesiastical jurisdiction in the external forum includes legislative, judicial and coactive power.[3]

[1] Ottaviani, *Compendium Iuris Publici Ecclesiastici*, n. 57; Wernz-Vidal, *Ius Canonicum*, II, n. 48.

[2] Canon 196.

[3] Canons 2220 and 2221.

The infliction of a canonical penalty is an act of jurisdiction in the external forum; hence it is evident that the laity who are incompetent to exercise ecclesiastical jurisdiction, and pastors who are restricted to the use of jurisdiction in the internal forum,[4] are not "lawful superiors" in the sense of canon 2222, § 1. It is equally evident that those who possess full power of jurisdiction as *ordinarii* are lawful superiors, authorized to inflict a proportionate penalty according to the prescript of this canon. Besides the Pope who possesses supreme jurisdiction over the entire Church, there are included residential bishops, vicars and prefects apostolic, abbots and prelates *nullius,* apostolic administrators, as well as the board of consultors and the vicar capitular during the vacancy of a see, and major superiors in clerical exempt orders.[5] Although the vicar-general is an ordinary, the Code expressly withdraws from his jurisdiction the power to inflict a penalty unless he has a special mandate from his superior.[6] It should be noted that the jurisdiction of all ordinaries is subject to any special restrictions made either in the common law or in the decrees of appointment.

Authors are not agreed concerning the lawful exercise of the special faculty by the *officialis* or the presiding judge of the diocesan court. Some authors[7] believe that the infliction of a canonical penalty without a previous warning in the case of notable scandal or of unusual gravity in the transgression is a legislative act and outside the competency of the superior who exercises only judicial power.[8] Other canonical writers interpret this special faculty as the simple application of an indeterminate canonical sanction established by the Code and inflicted according to canon 2223.[9] According to this inter-

[4] Canon 118.

[5] Canon 198.

[6] Canon 2220, § 2.

[7] D'Angelo, "Nozione del Delitto," *ETL,* III (1926), 213; Blat, *Commentarium Textus Codicis Iuris Canonici,* Lib. V, *De Delictis et Poenis* (Romae: Collegio "Angelico," 1924), n. 40; Roberti, *De Delictis et Poenis,* n. 53. p. 75.

[8] Canon 2220. Qui pollent... iudiciali tantum, possunt solummodo poenas, legitime statutas, ad norman iuris applicare.

[9] Michiels, *Normae Generales,* I, 204; *De Delictis et Poenis,* I, 81; Vermeersch-Creusen, *Epitome,* III, n. 412; Wernz-Vidal, *Ius Canonicum,* VII, n. 34, p. 176; Noval, "De Ratione Corrigendi," *Jus Pont.,* I-II (1921-1922), 154; Vidal, "Notio Delicti in Iure Codicis," *Jus Pont.,* III (1923), 100, 102; Coronata, *Institutiones,* IV, n. 1693.

pretation, the judicial powers of the presiding judge suffice for the inflicting of a proportionate penalty in a judicial trial in virtue of canon 2222, § 1.

D'Angelo was defending his theory of penal retroactivity when he asserted that legislative power is needed for the exercise of the special faculty granted in canon 2222, § 1, and therefore far exceeds the jurisdiction of the *officialis;*[10] Roberti rejects the theory of retroactivity but he admits: "Obstat, fatemur, . . .verbum *Superior* loco iudicis adhibitum. Si enim in can. 2222, § 1, agatur tantum de applicanda poena, non intelligitur cur eam iudex nequeat irrogare.[11]

It seems from the extrinsic authority of the canonical authors and the intrinsic authority of canonical reasoning that that opinion is preferable which does not restrict the lawful exercise of the special faculty mentioned in canon 2222, § 1, to those who possess legislative power. For both the terminology there used and the location of the canon in the Code argue for the inclusion of the *officialis* under the term *legitimus Superior.*[12]

Canon 2222, § 1, authorizes the lawful superior to impose *"aliqua iusta poena"*; thus the common law in facultative words establishes an indeterminate penalty which is to be imposed as a *ferendae sententiae* punishment. The subsequent canon directs: "Si lex in statuenda poena ferendae sententiae facultativis verbis utatur, committitur prudentiae et conscientiae

10 "Il caso adunque di una sanzione indeterminata contenuta nel dispositivo stesso é diversissimo da quello di una sanzione che manca affatto nella legge (proibente) ma che singula vice va aggiunta ed applicata: lì basta il potere giudiziario, qui si richiede anche il legislativo: ecco perchè non è il *Judex,* ma il *legitimus Superior* che può."—"Nozione del Delitto," *ETL,* III (1926), 213.

11 *De Delictis et Poenis,* n. 53, p. 75: however, the same author on another occasion appears to take the contrary view, for he says: "Principium 'nullum crimen sine lege' formaliter a Codice recipitur (c. 2195, § 1), sed sanctio potest esse valde indeterminata, immo *in iudicis facultate* posita (c. 2223, § 1), aut etiam statuere licet lex nullam sanctionem appositam habeat (c. 2222, § 1)."—"Respectus Sociales in Codice Iuris Canonici," *Appollinaris,* X (1937), 379. (Italics are inserted).

12 ". . .in societate ecclesiastica omnino non repugnat conferri Superiori, etiam legislativam potestatem non habenti, potestatem puniendi violationem legis non poenalis scandalosam vel peculiari modo gravem."—Vermeersch-Creusen, *Epitome,* III, n. 412.

iudicis eam infligere. . ."[13] Michiels points out[14] that the location of the canon under the title *"De Superiore potestatem coactivam habente"* is indicative of the fact that the *officialis* is in canon 2222, § 1, to be regarded as a *legitimus Superior,* for under this title canons 2220, § 1, and 2223 expressly speak of the infliction of penalties by those who possess *only judicial power.*[15] Furthermore, the codifier employs such expressions as *"poenas adnectere"* in canon 2220, § 1, and *"congrua poena munire"* in canon 2221, in order to indicate the need of legislative power; in contrast, the lawful superior mentioned in canon 2222, § 1, is one who is able *"aliqua iusta poena punire."*

The fundamental consideration however in seeking the solution to this difficulty is the canonical relationship that exists between the local ordinary and the judge. For the common law emphasizes[16] that it is the *ordinarius loci* who is the judge and who exercises this jurisdiction either *per se* or *per alios.* Although the bishop is bound to elect an *officialis* who is endowed with ordinary judicial power, the *officialis* can never exercise this office independently from the bishop; for the "officialis unum constituit tribunal cum Episcopo loci: sed nequit iudicare causas quas Episcopus sibi reservat."[17] Noval observed that whenever an ecclesiastical delict is judged and punished, it is always the superior acting either directly or indirectly through his *officialis* who exercises this jurisdiction. Consequently there is no reason to question the lawful use of the penal authority granted in canon 2222, § 1, by the *officialis.*

This dependency of the *officialis* on the bishop is accentuated in the legislation that concerns criminal trials, for in canons 1946, § 2, and 1954 the *officialis* is permitted to institute a criminal proceeding only with a special mandate from the ordinary. It was this consideration that moved Vidal to observe:

13 Canon 2223, § 2. (Italics are the writer's).

14 *Normae Generales,* I, 204.

15 It should be noted that in canons 1640, § 2; 1766, § 2, and 1845 the Code authorizes the presiding judge to annex penalties to precepts in the interest of preserving judicial order in the courts and of breaking down contumacy in the defendant and the witnesses. Cf. Vermeersch-Creusen, *Epitome,* III, n. 216.

16 Canon 1572, § 1.

17 Canons 1573; 1578.

> Ubi probe notandum est Codicem hoc loco [canon 2223] appellare *iudicem* vel *Superiorem*: nam licet pro causis iudicialibus iubeantur Ordinarii habere Officialem, nihilominus etiam in causis ad Officialem delatis Ordinarius est manetque iudex ordinarius, nec ab Officiali causae tractandae et decidendae sunt cum plena independentia ab Ordinario.[18]

It is the conclusion of the present writer that the term *legitimus Superior* and the phrase *poena punire* were inserted in canon 2222, § 1, with studied precision. For a *lawful superior* is a term so general as neither to require nor to exclude those who possess legislative power. The ordinary canonical procedure for punishing a delict is the judicial trial, wherein the judge imposes a proportionate penalty.[19] On the other hand, this general terminology allows for the extrajudicial application of the special faculty vindicated in canon 2222, § 1, when circumstances demand it. This opinion is supported by the use of the term *"poena punire,"* for, as Coronata says, it is a general phrase that can refer either to the *enactment* of a penalty, or to the *application* of a penalty, or to both.[20] Thus provision is made for both the judicial and the extrajudicial application of a canonical sanction in virtue of this canon.

It is evident that the major superior in a clerical exempt order may use the special authority accorded him in canon 2222, § 1;[21] it is disputed, however, whether the faculty is available to minor local superiors of a clerical exempt order.[22] Clancy defends the right of local superiors in clerical exempt

[18] *Ius Canonicum*, VII, n. 176.

[19] Canon 1933.

[20] "*Poenas infligere* et *poena punire* dictiones videntur quae de se tam ad poenae constitutionem quam ad poenae applicationem referri possunt et etiam ad utrumque simul. Poena stricte et proprie loquendo infligi dicitur cum. . . legis transgressio vi can. 2222, § 1, punitur. Qui poenam infligit non necessario iudex esse debet, saltem in iure Codicis."—*Institutiones*, IV, n. 1693, p. 87.

[21] Canon 198.

[22] Cfr. Vermeersch-Creusen, *Epitome*, III, n. 520; Clancy, *The Local Religious Superior*, The Catholic University of America Canon Law Studies, 175 (Washington, D. C.: The Catholic University of American Press, 1943), pp. 181 ss.

orders to apply penal sanctions in virtue of canon 2222, § 1, through an extrajudicial process unless the constitution of the order expressly restricts this right; in addition, if the local superior possesses delegated judicial power, he may impose a penalty in a judicial trial.[23] It seems that in each case the constitution of the individual exempt order must be studied if one is to determine the extent of the jurisdiction of minor local superiors.

ARTICLE II. THE JUDICIAL PROCESS

The special authority as granted in canon 2222, § 1, dispenses the lawful superior from the need of issuing a previous penal warning, and it permits that the violations in question be treated as true ecclesiastical delicts. It does not, however, dispense from the formalities of a criminal trial. It is a misconception of the nature of this canon to consider it as a procedural norm;[24] it is rather a penal canon that presupposes a system of canonical processes that are to be followed in the punishment of delicts.[25]

Canon 1933, § 1, establishes the ordinary and regular canonical rule that public ecclesiastical delicts are punished in a judicial trial.[26] Paragraph two of the same canon specifies the exceptions allowed by the lawgiver,[27] but the delicts that await punishment in virtue of the use of the special faculty mentioned in 2222, § 1, are not listed among the exceptions. From this it follows that ordinarily such delicts are subject to the usual rules of formal procedure.

23 *Op. cit.*, p. 18.

24 Rainer appears to fall into this error when he states: "Besides the exceptional course for which provision is made in canon 2222, § 1, there are two methods of inflicting a suspension. The one is by judicial sentence: the other is by a precept..."—*Suspension of Clerics*, The Catholic University of America Canon Law Studies, N. 111 (Washington, D. C.: The Catholic University of America, 1937), p. 151; Muñiz, *Procedimientos Eclesiásticos*, III, n. 544, p. 466.

25 "Sed putamus delictis esse accensendas transgressiones de quibus in c. 2222, § 1, nimirum quae non muniantur sanctione..."—Noval, "De Ratione Corrigendi," *Jus Pont.*, I-II (1921-1922), 148.

26 "Etenim loco huius propositionis (can. 1933, § 1) potest absdubio substitui: 'Delicta publica cadunt sub criminali iudicio.' "—Noval, "De Ratione Corrigendi," *Jus Pont.*, I-II (1921-1922), 150.

27 Canon 1933, § 2. Excipiuntur delicta plectenda sanctionibus poenalibus de quibus in can. 2168-2194.

However, it is important to note that canon 1933, § 1, speaks only of *public* delicts. A delict is public in the sense of canon 2197, 1°, when it is known to the people of a community or, when in view of the circumstances, it is prudently judged that it will be divulged. The direct antithesis of a public delict is the *occult* crime, from which it follows that a citation to appear for a judicial trial to answer for an occult delict could be ignored as invalid.[28] It may be that the superior is able to impose a punishment in such a case extrajudicially, but whether the delict must pass with impunity or not, occult crimes lie outside the canonical scope of the formal process.

Another factor that must be considered in the procedural aspects of canon 2222, § 1, is the *notoriety* of the violation.[29] Notoriety of fact exists when the delict is not only known to the community but also was committed under such circumstances that no subterfuge will suffice for concealing or excusing it. Proof of notoriety relieves the tribunal of the need to conduct a judicial investigation[30] and permits the superior to cite the delinquent and to proceed immediately to the imposition of some just penalty.[31] Rainer asserts that a notorious crime can be punished outside a judicial trial;[32] however, a notorious crime is not specifically different from a public crime in such a manner as to belong to a separate category of delicts.[33] Hence there is no reason for precluding notorious delicts from the regular norm that postulates a judicial process. There is no doubt that proof of notoriety greatly simplifies the formal trial in view of the lack of all further need to conduct a judicial investigation; but notoriety of itself does not obviate the need to observe the other judicial formalities.[34]

28 "Ad iudicium possunt deferri sola delicta publica, nullatenus delicta occulta, etiam probabilia, imo certa."—Noval, "De Ratione Corrigendi," *Jus Pont.*, I-II (1921-1922), 149, n. 5.

29 Canon 2197, 3°.

30 Canon 1747. Non indigent probatione: 1°. Facta notoria, ad normam can. 2197, nn. 2°, 3°.

31 Wernz-Vidal, *Ius Canonicum*, VI, 437; Ayrinhac-Lydon, *Penal Legislation*, n. 6; Roberti, *De Delictis et Poenis*, n. 44.

32 *Suspension of Clerics*, p. 152.

33 "Notorium est species publici, quia aliquid publico superaddit."—Robert, *De Delictis et Poenis*, n. 44.

34 ". . .hodie opportunissime notorietas arbitrio iudicis relinquitur aestimanda."—Roberti, *De Delictis et Poenis*, n. 44.

It will be seen in the next article that delicts which arise under the application of canon 2222, § 1, sometimes are subject to an extrajudicial process; nonetheless, the ordinary rule prevails that public ecclesiastical delicts are punished in a judicial trial. The fundamental reason for this rule of law is founded not only on the prescripts of the Code, but on the natural law itself which postulates a judicial process[35] whereby the rights of the accused are more securely safeguarded and the common good of society is more effectively defended.[36]

Muñiz (1874-1948) reluctantly agreed to the necessity of a formal trial in regard to public delicts that are punished by canon 2222, § 1.[37] He then proposed three different methods within the framework of the formal process by which delicts that arise through the application of canon 2222, § 1, can be brought to the ecclesiastical tribunal. He suggests that: 1) the ordinary may remand the judicial investigation as well as the determination and infliction of the proportionate penalty to the judge; or 2) the ordinary may relegate to the judge only the determination of the imputability and its gravity, reserving to himself the infliction of a proportionate sanction; or 3) the ordinary may determine a just penalty and order its infliction by the judge, if the tribunal finds guilt of a scandalous or grievous violation as postulated in canon 2222, § 1.[38] Any one of these three methods satisfies the general rule that public delicts must be punished in a formal trial, and they appear to correctly reflect the canonical relationship that exists between the local ordinary and his *officialis*.[39]

35 Bouix, *De Judiciis Ecclesiasticis* (2 vols., Parisiis, 1855), I, 16-17; Noval, "De Ratione Corrigendi," *Jus Pont.*, III (1923), 38; Vidal, "Notio Delictis in Iure Codicis," *Jus Pont.*, I (1921), 99.

36 "Quod iudicia in genere sint necessaria iure naturae... nam regulariter attentis studio partium et multiplicis generis passionibus, quae etiam in Superioribus vim exerunt et maxime cum agitur de coercendis delictis in particulari, sola iudicialis definitio... praebet moralem certitudinem de vera practica interpretatione legis poenalis et iuris delinquentis..."—Noval, "De Ratione Corrigendi," *Jus Pont.*, I-II (1921-1922), 151.

37 *Procedimientos Eclesiásticos,* III, n. 544, p. 466.

38 "Sin embargo, dando por bueno el parecer de tan illustre canonista, diremos que la transgresion escandolosa o muy grave de una ley que non tenga sanción canónica, podrá ser ilevada al tribunal eclesiástico de tres maneras: ..."—*Procedimientos Eclesiásticos,* III, n. 594, p. 466.

39 Canons 1572; 1573.

ARTICLE III. THE EXTRAJUDICIAL PROCESS

From a study of canon 1933, it is evident that the *ordinary* norm for punishing public delicts is the formal judicial trial.[40] However it would be a mistake to interpret this rule of law with such rigidity that the penal faculty as contained in canon 2222, § 1, would find no lawful application except in a formal process.[41] In the Code, the lawgiver has provided for both the judicial and the extrajudicial application of penalties. The penal authority that has been granted in canon 2222, § 1, is subject to application in either process according as it is warranted by the conditions that surround each individual case. This article will undertake a discussion of several of the more important questions that arise in connection with the extrajudicial application of a penalty in virtue of the authority enacted in canon 2222, § 1.

A. The Applicability of the Extrajudicial Process

Relative to the practical application of the extraordinary penal authority provided in canon 2222, § 1, several canonical writers are convinced that in accordance with its nature and character it is better adapted to use in the extrajudicial process than in a formal judicial trial.[42] Muñiz concedes that the ordinary rule as set forth in canon 1933, § 1, requires the judicial trial for public delicts;[43] but he points out that a special penal faculty is involved here which was enacted for use in certain cases that by their very nature may require immediate punitive action.

40 "Processus iudicialis de quo Codex loquitur in canonibus 1933 et sequentibus, est ordinaria ratio procedendi ad poenas infligendas vel declarandas."—Roberti, *De Delictis et Poenis*, n. 256; cf. also Coronata, *Manuale Practicum*, n. 25.

41 "Ergo licet ex iure naturali debet ex regula generali in omni societate completa iudiciorum proprie dictorum institutio induci: sed non ita urgere lex illa naturalis censenda est, ut non possit princeps ipse, et alii magistratus ab ipso constituti, in certis casibus iustitiam extraiudicialiter... exercere." —Bouix, *De Judiciis Ecclesiasticis*, I, 16-17.

42 "Nos parece que ese canon tiene mejor applicación en los procedimientos gubernativos pará castigar, que en los procedimientos judiciales."—Muñiz, *Procedimientos Eclesiásticos*, III, n. 544, p. 466; Coronata, "Pene e procedimenti 'ad modum praecepti'," *Perfice Munus*, VII (1932), 353.

43 *Loc. cit.*

It is true that the canon itself does not provide expressly for extrajudicial application. Nor is this surprising in view of the fact that this canon was not enacted as a procedural norm but as a penal norm. The legislator foregoes in this canon all terminology that would restrict the application of the special faculty within the framework of the formal process, and instead casts the canon in general terms that admit both a judicial and an extrajudicial application.[44]

The extraordinary character of the penal authority granted in this canon lends itself to an extrajudicial process. It is not an ordinary penal norm. The valid operation of the faculty is contingent upon the existence of extraordinary scandal or gravity in the transgression. It envisions a situation wherein the rights of society or the spiritual good of souls is jeopardized by peculiarly serious circumstances. The primary purpose of this norm is to provide a legal remedy to counteract the evil effects of notable scandal or of an unusually serious transgression; for this reason immediate punitive action may be necessary. In order to be efficacious, the infliction of a penalty under these circumstances may not permit delay; under such conditions, the right of the delinquent to the formalities of a judicial trial may be superseded by a higher right, so that at times the ordinary norm of canon 1933, § 1, is suspended by the moral impossibility of fulfillment.[45]

The fact that the legislator envisioned the extrajudicial application of this special penal faculty is evident from the position of this canon in relation to the provisions enacted under the same title in canon 2225.[46] Coronata points to the significance of this relationship and asserts that although the necessity of giving a previous penal warning has been relaxed in canon 2222, § 1, a penal sanction can be imposed *"per modum precepti"*.[47]

[44] Coronata, *Pene e Sanzioni Canoniche Estragiudiziali*, n. 23.

[45] Noval, "De Ratione Corrigendi," *Jus Pont.*, I-II (1921-1922), 151.

[46] "...si vero poena latae vel ferendae sententiae inflicta sit ad modum praecepti particularis scripto aut coram duobus testibus ordinarie declaretur vel irrogetur, indicatis poenae causis, salvo praescripto can. 2193."

[47] "Si potrebbe anche dire che tra il canone 2225 e 2222, § 1, vi è questa relazione. Il can. 2222, § 1, strettamente parlando non contiene alcuna pena determinata *a iure*, e percio non esclude la inflizione della pena a modo di precetto..."—*Pene e Sanzioni Canoniche Estragiudiziali*, n. 22.

It is for this reason that the legislator does not speak of a *iudex* in canon 2222, § 1, as he does in the following canon;[48] instead, it is the *legitimus Superior* who is authorized to exercise the special faculty enacted in the canon, a title that allows for both judicial and extrajudicial application of penal sanctions.[49]

Noval pointed to canon 1933, § 1 and § 2, where both the general rule for the necessity of a formal process and the lawful exceptions to this rule are constituted; he insisted that this enumeration of exceptions is complete and exclusive.[50] However he modified the rigidity of this rule with the following statement:

> Attamen, praeter eam, subaudienda est alia quae iure naturae et positivo divino viget de tuendo bono communi et animarum, videlicet, quod delicta publica non cadunt sub iudicio criminali quoties eorum deductio in iudicium est impossibilis aut noxia bono communi.[51]

It is evident from the extraordinary character of the legislative enactment of canon 2222, § 1 that the extrajudicial process in many cases will provide a more expeditious and effective vehicle for the reparation of specially serious scandal or gravity of transgression.

B. The Necessary Conditions

The circumstances that justify recourse to the extrajudicial process vary according as the delict is public or occult. However in every case where the penal authority enacted in canon 2222, § 1 is concerned, it is the physical or moral impossibility of holding a criminal trial that warrants the application of a canonical penalty *ad modum praecepti.*

48 Canon 2223, § 1. "In poenis applicandis iudex..."

49 "Si richiede prima de tutto il Superiore legittimo, Il Codice non parla di giudice, ma de Superiore; ciò non esclude che anche et giudice possa pigliare simili provedimenti, specialmente quando si tratta di giudice che e nello stesso tempo Superiore legittimo."—Coronata, "Pene e procedimenti 'ad modum praecepti'," *Perfice Munus,* VII (1932), 353.

50 "...nulla alia potest a quopiam infra ipsum superaddi."—"De Ratione Corrigendi," *Jus Pont.,* I-II (1921-1922), 152.

51 *Loc. cit.*

When the delict that is under consideration is a *public* delict, the circumstances that allow the lawful use of the extrajudicial process are to be found in parallel canons. In the extraordinary penal process known as *suspensio ex informata conscientia*[52] the supreme lawgiver has dispensed both from the need of giving a previous warning and from the formalities of a judicial trial. The legislation that was enacted relative to this process specifies three sets of circumstances under which a *public* delict may be punished outside the formal process.[53]

1. the refusal of witnesses to give testimony that is essential to the prosecution of a case in a formal trial;
2. the impossibility of instituting formal proceedings in consequence of the malice of the delinquent;
3. the formal process is impeded because of adverse secular laws or from the danger of aggravated scandal that might emerge from a public judicial trial.[54]

Whenever one or more of these conditions are verified, the superior is justified in adopting the extrajudicial process for inflicting a proportionate penalty against a delict that arises under the application of the special faculty granted in canon 2222, § 1. For in such a case, the use of the formal trial is either physically or morally impossible. The primary purpose

[52] Canons 2186-2194.

[53] Canon 2191, § 3.

[54] Cf. Cappello, "Irrogatio poenae per modum praecepti extra iudicium," *Periodica de Re Canonica et Morali utili Praesertim Religiosis et Missionariis,* XIX (1930), 36-38. Cappello relies on canon 2191, §3, 3°, to extend the general preceptive power of inflicting penalties beyond the limits as set forth in canon 1933, § 4. This writer does not agree that such an extension is warranted in its application to an ordinary norm for inflicting penalties. For suspension *ex informata conscientia* was enacted as an *extraordinary* penal remedy and any extension of its provisions so as to apply to the ordinary extrajudicial process does not seem to be justified.

However this objection cannot be alleged validly against the application of canon 2191, § 3, to the penal authority granted in canon 2222, § 1; for between these two penal norms there exists an intimate canonical relationship. Both are extraordinary in character inasmuch as they demonstrate the lawful infliction of a canonical penalty without previous warning. It is for this reason that several authors point to suspension *ex informata conscientia* as an example of the application of the special penal faculty contained in canon 2222, § 1. Cf. Vermeersch-Creusen, *Epitome,* III, n. 412; Ayrinhac-Lydon, *Penal Legislation,* n. 40.

of all coercive action is the safeguarding of the public order; if a formal trial would frustrate this end, the extrajudicial process should be employed.[55]

There is also a direct parallel between the canons of the Code that provide for the immediate and extrajudicial dismissal of a religious by the minor local superior when the common good of the community is endangered by specially serious scandal or the extraordinary gravity of the transgression on the part of a delinquent.[56]

If the delict is *occult* in nature[57] and in the judgment of the superior the infliction of a penalty is necessary, the use of the extrajudicial process is mandatory. For in consequence of the ruling in canon 1933, § 1, occult delicts lie outside the competency of a formal process. It is evident that an especially grievous crime could at the same time remain occult in the sense of canon 2197, 4°; furthermore, the terms *scandalous* and *occult* are not necessarily antithetical in their connotations.[58] Therefore if an occult violation of a non-penal law incurs a delictual imputability in accordance with the requirements of canon 2222, § 1, the lawful superior may impose a proportionate penalty extrajudicially.

The extrajudicial infliction of a canonical penalty in consequence of the authority granted in this canon presupposes two essential elements: first, that the penalty will not be imposed until the defendant has had a hearing and has been given an adequate opportunity to defend his innocence. This prescript of the natural law is not subject to dispensation by any human authority;[59] secondly, the superior must have gathered proof

[55] "...salus aeterna animae, sive delinquentium sive ceterorum, quae est scopus poenae frustraretur si processus iudicialis servari deberet."—Noval, "De Ratione Corrigendi," *Jus Pont.*, III (1923), p. 205, n. 12.

[56] Canons 653 and 668.

[57] Canon 2197, 4°. *Occultum,* quod non est publicum; *occultum materialiter,* si lateat delictum ipsum; *occultum formaliter,* si eiusdem imputabilitas.

[58] "Quare occultum potest esse crimen quod a nonnullis scitur a quibus tamen non est timenda evulgatio. In his potius quam numerus attendenda est qualitas personarum."—Roberti, *De Delictis et Poenis,* n. 44.

[59] "Ante omnia autem ius naturale praecipit ut reo damnando iusta defensio concedatur, nec inauditus damnetur."—Coronata, *Manuale Practicum,* n. 27; *Institutiones,* IV, n. 1711; Roberti, *De Delictis et Poenis,* n. 263.

that will substantiate three facts: 1) that a delict has been committed;[60] 2) that it is morally imputable to the defendant;[61] and 3) that notabile scandal or special gravity is involved in the transgression.[62]

Again it is noted that the ecclesiastical superior has no obligation to prosecute and punish every delict that arises in consequence of the penal norm granted in canon 2222, § 1. Occasionally, prudence will dictate a course of action that involves neither the judicial or extrajudicial infliction of a penalty. Nevertheless, when the superior deems it necessary in the interests of the common good to inflict a penal sanction, the extrajudicial process is available to him under circumstances that render impossible a formal criminal trial.

C. The Necessary Formalities

The extrajudicial process in which a penalty is imposed points to nothing more than an executive order[63] issued by the competent superior to the defendant in which the prescript of canon 2225 is observed.[64] It is called an *executive process* for the reason that no precept containing a threat of punishment preceded; in this way it is distinguished from the canonical process enacted in canon 1933, § 4 which implies the issuance of two precepts: one given *ad instar legis* which threatens a

60 "Non sufficerent proinde ad poenam infligendam per modum praecepti argumenta plus minusve probabilia contra reum..."—Coronata, *Manuale Practicum,* n. 28.

61 "Non tantum requiritur certitudo de facto delictuoso a reo commisso, sed omnino etiam requiritur certitudo de eius dolo seu culpabilitate seu imputabilitate delinquentis."—Coronata, *op. cit.,* n. 28.

62 "Quod si Superior certus sit de delicto a subdito commisso, sed hanc certitudinem ex mera scientia privata habeat... non debet pariter ad poenam infligendam procedere, quia eius decretum in casu recursus facile posset a Sancta Sede irritari, licet per se validum habendum sit."—Coronata, *op. cit.,* n. 28; Vermeersch-Creusen, *Epitome,* III, n. 377.

63 "Alter potest dici processus exsecutorius, seu absque praevia poenae comminatione... est emendatorius, quando ei causam praebet legis transgressio specialiter gravis; punitivus seu vindicativus, si causam praebet notabile scandalum."—Noval, "De Ratione Corrigendi," *Jus Pont.,* III (1923), 205.

64 "...si vero poena latae vel ferendae sententiae inflicta sit ad modum praecepti particularis, scripto aut coram duobus testibus ordinarie declaretur vel irrogetur..."

penalty and a subsequent precept given *ad instar sententiae* which actually inflicts the threatened penalty.[65]

The special penal faculty in canon 2222, § 1, essentially consists in the authorization to inflict a penalty without the issuance of a previous warning; Noval correctly pointed out[66] that this authorization necessarily implies a dispensation from the observance of the ordinary process which requires the issuance of a warning penal precept given *ad instar legis.*[67]

From this, it can be seen that the extrajudicial infliction of penalty in this case is a simplified version of the ordinary *per modum praecepti* process as provided in canon 1933, § 4. However this does not imply that the process is completely arbitrary. The primary purpose of all judicial formalities is the safeguarding of the rights of the defendant and the prevention of a possible miscarriage of justice. The foregoing of these formalities entails a greater responsibility for the superior who proceeds extrajudicially.[68]

There exists no one, well-defined formula that must be followed when a canonical penalty is inflicted in the extrajuicial process, but the prescripts of law given in canons 24 and 2225 should be observed.

If the superior elects to inflict the penalty orally, he should summon the defendant and in the presence of two canonically suitable witnesses inform the defendant that he has incurred a definite penalty, giving the reasons for inflicting it. Either a notary or one of the witnesses should put this in writing

65 Noval, "De Ratione Corrigendi," *Jus Pont.*, I-II (1921-1922), 155-156; Coronata, *Pene e Sanzioni Canoniche Estragiudiziali,* n. 8; Sole, *De Delictis et Poenis,* nn. 102, 103.

66 "De Ratione Corrigendi," *Jus Pont.*, III (1923), n. 9, 38-39.

67 "Da ciò si può dedurre che questo modo di punire è più semplice ancora che quello stabilito nel can. 1933, § 4, di cui si è parlato sopra. Per imporre infatti una sanzione penale a modo di precetto è necessario che si premetta il precetto stesso contenente pena specifica *latae o ferendae sententiae;* qui invece si può procedere all' inflizione della pena senza necessità di premettere nè il precetto nè la comminazione di una pena determinata."—Coronata, *Pene e Sanzioni Canoniche Estragiudiziali,* n. 22.

68 "Equidem, si etiam in iudicio, auditis et discussis in contradictorio accusatione et allegationibus promotoris iustitiae, et excusationibus ac defensionibus tum rei cum eius advocati, servatisque aliis rigidioribus normis, non est negotium facile definire in concreto delictum et determinare poenam, absdubio erit difficilius utrumque perficere extraiudicialiter."—Noval, "De Ratione Corrigendi," *Jus Pont.*, III (1923), 205.

and this document should be signed by the superior, the defendant and the two witnesses.

If no witnesses are present, the superior can draw up a document in which the penalty and its cause are contained; after the precept has been read to the defendant, both the superior and the defendant should sign the document.

Perhaps the most practical method for inflicting a canonical penalty is by way of an official document. It is either delivered personally to the defendant by the superior or a duly constituted messenger or through the public mails. If the document is sent through the public mails, it should be registered to be delivered to the addressee personally, with a request for a return receipt.[69]

If the penalty is imposed by means of a legal document, it should contain the essential facts: the name of the delinquent, the competent superior, the delict that involves extraordinary scandal or gravity and the specific penal sanction invoked; a notation of the place, the day, the month and the year together with the signatures of the superior and the notary under seal should be added.

Irregardless of the method employed to impose a penalty, an authentic copy of the decree should always be retained in the archives.[70]

The observance of these formalities provides evidence that the penalty has been lawfully imposed. If later on it becomes necessary to enforce the penalty in the external forum, the necessary proofs are at hand. In addition the observance of these formalities entails the duration of the penalty beyond the term of incumbency on the part of the superior who inflicted it; and if the delinquent seeks redress against the penalty, this evidence of the valid infliction of the penalty together with the proofs of the delictual guilt can be forwarded to the Holy See.[71]

69 Coronata, *Manuale Practicum,* n. 30.

70 Coronata, *op. cit.,* n. 30.

71 Canon 24.

CHAPTER EIGHT

THE LAWFUL PENALTY

The competent superior is authorized in canon 2222, § 1, to impose "some just penalty" for violations of law and precept that fall within the ambit of the special penal authority.[1] The etymological source of the word *iusta* goes back to the Latin words for law and justice (*ius* and *iustitia*);[2] consequently a *iusta poena* as authorized by this canon is one that is determined in accordance to the principles of law and justice.[3] Hence a *poena iusta* is one that conforms to the prescripts of law and evinces an equitable proportion between the delictual imputability and the penalty imposed by the competent superior. This final chapter will be devoted to a consideration of the various canonical principles involved in the determination of a lawful penalty.

From the canon itself it is evident that the undetermined penalty is to be imposed as a *ferendae sententiae* punishment; for a *latae sententiae* penalty presupposes a full determination of its nature by the legislator in the law itself at the time of its promulgation.[4] It is important to note also that the threatened penalty as implied in canon 2222, § 1, is stated in facultative terms,[5] which fact gives to the superior an option for inflicting or withholding the penalty in a given case according as the circumstances demand.[6]

[1] Canon 2222, § 1: "...legitimus tamen Superior potest aliqua iusta poena punire..."

[2] Cicognani, *Canon Law,* pp. 8-10

[3] "Fundamentum cuiuslibet poenae nequit esse nisi *iustitia*... at auctoritas humana in ferendis poenis nequit praescindere a iustitia absoluta Dei, cuius legibus et ipsa tenetur, quia potestas delegata iuxta normam statutam a delegante est exercenda."—Roberti, *De Delictis et Poenis,* n. 32.

[4] Canon 2217, §1, 1° and 2°.

[5] "...potest...aliqua iusta poena punire..."

[6] Canon 2223, § 2. Si lex in statuenda poena ferendae sententiae facultativis verbis utatur, committitur prudentiae et conscientiae iudicis eam infligere...

ARTICLE I. LIMITATIONS IMPOSED BY CANON 1933, § 4

A factor of decisive importance in the determination of a lawful penalty is the nature of the process employed to inflict the punishment. For if the *extrajudicial* process is used, the legislator has indicated in canon 1933, § 4, that the ecclesiastical superior is restricted to imposing one of five different canonical penalties: a canonical penance, penal remedy, excommunication, suspension or interdict.[7] It is the opinion of this writer that this is an exclusive enumeration of the canonical penalties that are available to the superior when he imposes a penalty extrajudicially in virtue of the special faculty granted in canon 2222, § 1.[8] If the superior wishes to inflict a penalty other than one of those listed in canon 1933, § 4, the formal criminal process appears to be mandatory.

It is true that no authentic interpretation of canon 1933 has been forthcoming, and there is an impressive group of canonical writers who support a far more liberal opinion concerning the extension of this canon.[9] In fact, Roberti holds that unless the law expressly demands the use of the judicial process in inflicting a particular penal sanction, every canonical penalty is subject to extrajudicial application.[10] However his arguments in support of this interpretation are not convincing.

His principle defense of this opinion is an appeal to the practice of the curias both before and after the Code. The sweeping abrogation of penal law contained in canon 6, 5°, appears to invalidate any argument based on the pre-Code practice. Nor would the practice of the curias since the Code, in itself, justify this extensive interpretation of canon 1933, § 4. It is a question here of seeking a canonical interpretation which

[7] "Considerato il canone 1933, § 4, dove si enumerano le pene che possono essere inflitte estragiudizialmente, bisogna dire che se il Superiore vuole procedere in questo caso extragiudizialmente deve limitarsi ad applicare le pene ivi enumerate.

Se quindi il Superiore ecclesiastico vuole procedere all' applicazione di altre pene oltre quelle enumerate nel can. 1933, § 4, dovrà adattarsi a seguire la forma giudiziaria."—Coronata, *Pene e Sanzioni Canoniche Estragiudiziali,* n. 23

[8] Cf. also Noval, "De Ratione Corrigendi,"—*Jus Pont.,* I-II (1921-1922), 155-156.

[9] Cf. Roberti, *De Delictis et Poenis,* nn. 259-262 for an exposition of the four leading opinions concerning this problem and their respective exponents.

[10] *Op. cit.,* n. 262.

conforms with the mind of the lawgiver as expressed in the law rather than an interpretation which conforms to a practice which possibly is an abuse.[11]

The wording of canon 1933, § 4, clearly does not demand a more comprehensive interpretation than that endorsed by this writer. In fact if every canonical penalty is available for the *per modum preçepti* process, as Roberti asserts, the enumeration of the five penalties in 1933, § 4, would seem to serve no purpose whatsoever. It would have been very easy for the lawgiver to have expressed his intention of sharing with subordinate superiors the authority to inflict all penalties by way of the extrajudicial process.[12] The absence of any such expression argues for the unlawfulness of any interpretation or practice that extends the extrajudicial coercive powers of local superiors.

Roberti himself concedes that this strict interpretation is in close conformity to the penal laws of the Code.[13] For, as a penal law, it is subject to strict interpretation[14] and in case of doubt concerning the lawful extension of its authority, that interpretation must be considered as preferable which is less extensive. For this reason the enumeration of penalties in canon 1933, § 4, should be considered as complete and exclusive.[15] Consequently whenever a penalty is imposed extrajudicially in virtue of the authority enacted in canon 2222, § 1, the character and nature of that penalty will be restricted by the prescript of canon 1933, § 4.[16]

ARTICLE II. THE VINDICATIVE CHARACTER OF THE PENALTY

A study of the nature and purpose of the special penal faculty constituted in canon 2222, § 1, indicates that the legis-

[11] Esswein, *Extrajudicial Coercive Powers of Ecclesiastical Superiors,* p. 113.

[12] Canon 2291. "Poenae vindicative... *praesertim* sunt,"; Canon 2313: "*Praecipuae* poenitentiae sunt..." (Italics are inserted).

[13] "Haec interpretatio est stricta et bene respondet legibus poenalibus. Etenim processus in quo maxima cautio in administranda iustitia residet, non est dispensandus nisi expresse dicatur. Iam vero dispensatio ultra limites supra descriptos saltem est dubia; ergo non est admittenda."—*De Delictis et Poenis,* n. 259.

[14] Canon 19.

[15] Canons 19; 2119, § 1.

[16] "Poenitentia, remedium poenale, excommunicatio, suspensio, interdictum, dummodo delictum certum sit, infligi possunt etiam per modum praecepti extra iudicium."

lator did not contemplate the use of censures and that the penal power therein granted is restricted to the use of vindicative penalties.[17]

The lawful exercise of the special faculty is permitted only when the scandal caused by the violation is more than ordinarily serious or when the gravity of the transgression is in some way intensified. This indicates that the legislator is more concerned over the need of reparation for the scandal and of atonement for the grievous transgression than with the amendment of the delinquent.[18] It is this primary effect when sought through punitive action that distinguishes the vindicative from the medicinal penalty.

The lawful imposing or inflicting of a censure presupposes not only a grave violation of law but also a formal contempt for the authority that enacted the law.[19] The Code makes it clear that contumacy is not presumed; it must stand certified through proof upon the previous use of a specific admonition.[20] Therefore, when the lawgiver authorizes the inflicting of a penalty *"sine praevia poena comminatione,"* it is to be presumed that a vindicative rather than medicinal penalty is to be employed. To argue that the canon dispenses the superior from the need of issuing a previous warning before he imposes a censure is equivalent to saying that the lawgiver has dispensed from the need of having proof that contumacy exists; yet, without possession of this proof the use of the censure is never justified.

The very fact that the superior in his use of the special faculty which canon 2222, § 1, grants him can abstract from the need of issuing a specific prior warning indicates the vindicative purpose of the penalties imposed in consequence of the

[17] Michiels, *Normae Generales,* I, 202; Noval, "De Ratione Corrigendi," *Jus Pont.,* III (1923), 39; Coronata, *Institutiones,* IV, n. 1695; Beste, *Introductio in Codicem,* p. 891; Wernz-Vidal, *Ius Canonicum,* VII, n. 34; Vermeersch-Creusen, *Epitome,* III, n. 412; Blat, *De Delictis et Poenis,* n. 40; Berutti, *Institutiones Iuris Canonici,* VI, 75.

[18] Canon 2286.

[19] Canon 2241, § 1. "Censura est poena qua homo baptizatus, delinquens et contumax..."; Ayrinhac-Lydon, *Penal Legislation,* n. 75.

[20] Canon 2233, § 2. "Licet id legitime constet, si agatur de infligenda censura, reus reprehendatur ac moneatur...; contumacia persistente, censura infligi potest"; cfr. canon 2242, § 2.

superior's use of this extraordinary power.[21] This interpretation does not preclude all possible use of censures against violations of non-penal juridic norms; such a violation can become the occasion for a penal precept which threatens a censure in the event of failure to amend and to atone for the scandal.[22] However, this course of action falls not within the scope of the special faculty of the canon, but within the general preceptive power of the superior.[23]

The opinion which permits the use of both medicinal and vindicative penalties is not lacking in probability,[24] and it can be followed. But once again the principle of strict interpretation is applicable, for the censure is considered the more serious and grave of the two penalties. It seems that the exclusive use of vindicative penalties in connection with the use of the special faculty reflects greater conformity to this principle.[25]

In this connection, it should be noted that excommunication and personal interdict are always of a medicinal character,[26] and, in accordance with this stricter opinion, they should not be used unless a previous warning has been issued.

ARTICLE III. THE SEVERITY OF THE PENALTY

As several canonical writers mention, the proportionate penalty authorized in canon 2222, § 1, is not one of the more severe penal sanctions constituted in the Code.[27] This

21 Noval, "De Ratione Corrigendi," *Jus Pont.*, III (1923), 39.

22 "Ora nel can. 2222, § 1 non si esime il Superiore dall' osservare il can. 1933, § 4, e tanto meno dal can. 2225. Certamente se il Superiore impone per pena una censura, dovrà in qualche modo preavvertire il reo, e.g., comandandoli una riparazione dello scandalo sotto la pena di incorrere la censura. Lo scandalo potrà qualche volta essere riparato anche coll' accettazione di una buona penitenza."—Coronata, *Pene e Sanzioni Canoniche Estragiudiziali*, n. 24, note 141 bis.

23 Wernz-Vidal, *Ius Canonicum*, VII, n. 34; Coronata, *Institutiones*, IV, n. 1695.

24 "Since the terminology of canon 2222, § 1, is of a general nature, it can be said that not only a vindictive penalty but also a censure may be inflicted, according as the circumstances require."—Esswein, *Extrajudicial Coercive Powers of Ecclesiastical Superiors*, p. 119; Rainer, *Suspension of Clerics*, p. 125.

25 Canon 19.

26 Coronata, *Institutiones*, IV, n. 1783; canons 2255, § 2 and 2291.

27 "Poena est 'aliqua... poena,' minor quam graves poenae in delicta iure definita statutae..."—Vermeersch-Creusen, *Epitome*, III, n. 412; Ayrinhac-Lydon, *Penal Legislation*, n. 40; Noval, "De Ratione Corrigendi," *Jus Pont.*, III (1923), 39.

interpretation is founded on the pre-Code practice in the use of extraordinary penalties as well as on the law of the Code, and it finds support in arguments drawn from reasonable assumptions.

The use of extraordinary penalties before the Code was discussed earlier.[28] These *poenae arbitrariae* were employed against violations of non-penal laws,[29] but with the present codification of the Church's law their use has become restricted within the scope of the special faculty granted in canon 2222, § 1. Pre-Code commentators however mentioned the fact that, when these extraordinary penal sanctions were invoked, their severity as a rule was not to transcend that of the ordinary penalties as determined in the law.[30] This pre-Code practice must be considered when a canonical penalty is inflicted through the application of the special faculty authorized in canon 2222, § 1.[31]

To a large extent, however, the legislator has already provided for this consideration through the insertion of reserve clauses which with reference to the more serious canonical penalties permit their infliction only against certain specified delicts. Among the more grave penalties that may not be employed by the superior in his use of the extraordinary power which canon 2222, § 1, grants him are deposition,[32] perpetual or even temporary deprivation of the clerical garb,[33] degradation,[34] *infamia iuris*,[35] and the penal deprivation of a benefice if its holder is an irremovable incumbent.[36] There are other

28 Chapter III, art. 3, p. 23.

29 C. 4, X, *de officio et potestate judicis delegati*, I, 29.

30 "Unde quotiescunque poena erit arbitraria, judex... per se debet inclinare in mitiorem partem, nisi reus esset solitus delinquere."—Reiffenstuel, *Ius Canonicum Universum*, V, tit. 37, nn. 10, 11; Ried-Brig, *Manuale Practicum Iuris Disciplinaris et Criminalis* (Romae: Typis Vaticanis, 1902), pp. 13 and 111.

31 Canon 6, 3°. "Poenae autem extraordinariae debebant esse minores quam illae ordinariae, et etiam hodie et semper debent esse minores."—Noval, "De Ratione Corrigendi," *Jus Pont.*, III (1923), 39.

32 Canon 2303, § 3.

33 Canons 2304 and 2300.

34 Canon 2305.

35 Canon 2293, § 2.

36 Canon 2299, § 1.

penalties, such as those which involve some kind of disability, that are very restrictively applicable according to the provisions of the law.[37]

Some of the factors which surround the infliction of a penalty through the application of the special faculty granted in canon 2222, § 1, support the interpretation that the penalty should be less severe than the penalty ordinarily designated in the law. By its very nature it is an extraordinary penalty inasmuch as the usual norm presupposes at least the embodiment of an indeterminate sanction in each individual law or precept. Then, too, the determination of both the delict and the penalty is left to the prudent judgment of the superior, so that the delinquent has at most an imperfect knowledge of the penalty to which he is subject. The Code recognizes this as a factor that lessens, though it does not completely cancel out, delictual imputability.[38]

Relative to this consideration it should be remembered however that the lawgiver does provide in canon 2222, § 1, a general penal warning that especially scandalous or unusually grievous violations of non-penal laws are subject to coercive measures. Similarly the fact that the penalty is undetermined is not of decisive importance, since this indetermination conforms to the general policy of canonical penal sanctions. Some authors suggest that in the use of the special faculty granted in canon 2222, § 1, the opportunity of self-defense is lessened, and therefore the inflicted penalty should be milder in its character.[39] However this argument, in the opinion of the present writer, carries little force; for irregardless of the process that is employed, the defendant has a right to an adequate defense of his innocence. For even in the extrajudicial process, a superior would act unlawfully unless he granted the defendant full opportunity to defend his rights[40] and notwithstanding this,

37 Canon 2296.

38 Canon 2202, § 2. Ignorantia solius poenae imputabilitatem delicti non tollit, sed aliquantum minuit.

39 "The reason for less severe penalties is that the delinquent had no way of previously knowing the penalty to which he was liable... also because there was not given to him the opportunity to defend himself, as would be granted under ordinary conditions."—Esswein, *Extrajudicial Coercive Powers of Ecclesiastical Superiors*, p. 119; Noval, "De Ratione Corrigendi," *Ius Pont.*, III (1923) 39.

40 Roberti, *De Delictis et Poenis*, n. 263.

unmistakable proof of the certain and imputable commission of the delict is at hand.[41]

All of these considerations however have merit in varying degrees and should play a part in the actual determination of a proportionate penalty imposed under the extraordinary authority of this canon. Nonetheless the decisive factor must be the efficacious attainment of the primary purpose of the faculty: to provide a penal norm for the reparation of notable scandal and of the special gravity in the transgression.[42]

Among the penalties suggested as applicable under this special authority are public rebuke or admonition,[43] the refusal of a vacation, suspension from one's office or the exercise of one's orders, or the payment of a moderate pecuniary fine. The command or the prohibition to reside in a specified place is considered a grave and severe penalty, and it should be used only when it is considered necessary as a means of reparation for very serious scandal or for the unusual gravity manifest in the transgression.[44] Ayrinhac—Lydon suggest the penal transfer from an office or benefice to one of lesser importance.[45] There seems to be no reason for excluding even the *penal deprivation* of a benefice or office from the canonical penalties applicable under this special faculty as long as the defendant is a removable incumbent. The Code requires a *causa rationabilis;*[46] however, ordinarily it appears advisable to follow the administrative process provided by the common law for removing a removable pastor from his parish.[47]

The lawgiver has rightly left the actual determination of the penalty to the prudent judgment of the local superior who alone is in a position to evaluate the various factors which it is essential to duly appraise if he is to achieve an equitable proportion between the delict and the penalty. This evaluation

41 Canon 2233, § 1.

42 "In poenis decernendis servetur aequa proportio cum delicto, habita ratione imputabilitatis, scandali et damni..."—Canon 2218, § 1.

43 Coronata, *Institutiones,* IV, n. 1824; canons 2291 and 2298.

44 Canon 2302.

45 *Penal Legislation,* n. 40.

46 Canon 2299, § 1.

47 Canons 2157-2161.

however must be based upon and in conformity with the general principles of penal law as discussed in this chapter. If a question arises concerning the justice of a penalty that has been imposed, the presumption of law favors the judgment of the superior until the contrary is established through conclusive proof.[48]

If the delinquent seeks redress, either by way of appeal or through the interposition of a recourse against the penalty that has been imposed in virtue of the extraordinary faculty of this canon, his action suspends the execution of the vindicative penalty while the appeal or the recourse is pending.[49]

[48] Canon 2219, § 2. At si dubitetur utrum poena, a Superiore competente inflicta, sit iusta, necne, poena servanda est in utroque foro, excepto casu appellationis in suspensivo.

[49] Canon 2287. Ab inflictis poenis vindicativis datur appellatio seu recursus in suspensivo, nisi aliud expresse in iure caveatur. Cf. also canon 1889, § 2. However in many canons of the Code, the law expressly withdraws the right to *suspensive* recourse: cf. canons 345; 512; 513; 880, § 2; 1340; 1395; 1428; 2146.

CONCLUSIONS

1. From the fourth century onward, the development of a penal and procedural system in ecclesiastical law manifested a definite trend towards regulation and restriction in the use of coercive power. However, adequate discretionary authority was always provided for cases that were attended with serious scandal or a special gravity in the transgression.

2. At least three distinct but closely inter-related juridic concepts underlie the principle *nulla poena sine lege.* Evident traces of the development of these fundamental penal concepts are found in the sources of ecclesiastical jurisprudence.

3. Tridentine legislation demonstrated the lawfulness of inflicting a canonical penalty apart from a specific previous warning in certain occasional circumstances. The special faculty as granted in canon 2222, § 1, represents a general extension of this aspect of penal procedure.

4. Pre-Code penal law provided for the application of extraordinary penalties in violations of non-penal laws. The special authority enshrined in canon 2222, § 1, represents a residuum of that discretionary penal authority. In the penal law of the Code, the lawful extent of this discretionary penal power stands confined within the scope of this canon.

5. The principle if not the formula *nulla poena sine lege* has been canonized in the present legislation of the Code. The special faculty granted in canon 2222, § 1, does not constitute an exception to this principle nor does it neutralize its canonical efficacy.

6. The definition of a delict in canon 2195 does not postulate the *incorporation* of a penal clause in each individual juridic norm. It does require that the threat of at least an indeterminate penalty precede the violation. For this reason no real conflict in principle exists between the provisions of canons 2195 and 2222, § 1. The juridical element that is essential to

the nature of an ecclesiastical delict is supplied by canon 2222, § 1, wherein a proportionate penalty is threatened for the violation of any non-penal law or precept that involves notable scandal or a special gravity in the transgression.

7. The special penal faculty that is authorized in canon 2222, § 1, does not establish a general *juridic* obligation in virtue of which scandal can be punished wherever or whenever it emerges. Rather, the lawful exercise of this special authority presupposes the violation of some non-penal law to which the delinquent was juridically held; in addition the use of the faculty postulates as a *conditio sine qua non* that the violation was accompanied by a more than ordinarily serious scandal or a special gravity in the transgression.

8. The general terminology employed in canon 2222, § 1, abstracts from any and all requirement of legislative power in the lawful superior who exercises the special authority granted in the canon. The canon does not essentially deal with the problem of procedure; it leaves room for both a judicial and an extrajudicial procedure in its application and use.

9. It rests with the prudent judgment of the lawful superior to determine when the scandal or the violation is extraordinarily serious as well as to determine the proportionate penalty. From the nature of the special authority granted in canon 2222, § 1, it appears that only vindicative penalties should be inflicted, and ordinarily they should be less severe than the penalties designated in the law. Nonetheless the superior is authorized to impose a penalty which serves adequately to atone for the serious scandal or the particular gravity of the violation.

BIBLIOGRAPHY

SOURCES

Acta Apostolicae Sedis, Commentarium Officiale, Romae, 1909—

Acta Sanctae Sedis, 41 vols., Romae, 1865-1908.

Bouscaren, T. Lincoln, *The Canon Law Digest,* 2 vols., Milwaukee, Wis.: Bruce Publishing Co., 1934-1943.

Bruns, H. T., *Canones Apostolorum et Conciliorum Saeculorum IV-VII,* 2 vols., Berolini, 1839.

Codex Iuris Canonici Pii X Pontificis Maximi iussu digestus Benedicti Papae XV auctoritate promulgatus, praefatione, fontium annotatione et indice analytico—alphabetico ab Emo Petro Card. Gasparri auctus, Romae: Typis Polyglottis Vaticanis, 1917.

Codicis Iuris Canonici Fontes, cura Emi Petri Card. Gasparri editi, 9 vols., Romae (postea Civitate Vaticana): Typis Polyglottis Vaticanis, 1923-1939 (Vols. VII-IX, ed. cura et studio Emi Iustiniani Card. Serédi.).

Collectanea S. Congregationis de Propaganda Fide, 2 vols., Romae: Typographia Polyglotta S. C. de Propaganda Fide, 1907.

Corpus Iuris Canonici, ed. Lipsiensis secunda, post Aemilii Ludovici Richteri curas... instruxit Aemilius Friedberg, 2 vols., Lipsiae: Tauchnitz, 1879-1881: ed. anatastice repetita, 1928.

Corpus Scriptorum Ecclesiasticorum Latinorum, 68 vols., Vindobonae, 1866-

Decretales D. Gregorii IX una cum Glossis Restitutae, Romae, 1582.

Decretum Gratiani, emendatum et notationibus illustratum, una cum glossis, 2 vols., Romae, 1582.

Hardouin, Jean, *Acta Conciliorum et Epistolae Decretales ac Constitutiones Summorum Pontificum,* 12 vols., Parisiis, 1714-1715.

Jaffé, Philippus, *Regesta Pontificum Romanorum ab condita Ecclesia ad annum post Christum natum MCXCVIII,* 2. ed., G. Wattenbach, F. Kaltenbrunner, P. Ewald, S. Loewenfeld, 2 vols., Lipsiae, 1885-1888.

Liber Sextus Decretalium D. Bonifacii Papae VIII suae integritati una cum Clementinis et Extravagantibus earumque Glossis restitutis, Romae 1582.

Mansi, J. D., *Sacrorum Conciliorum Nova et Amplissima Collectio,* 53 vols., Paris-Arnhem-Leipzig, 1901-1927.

Monumenta Germaniae Historica, 188 vols., incompleta, Hannoverae,—*Leges,* 5 vols., Vols. I-IV ed. G. Pertz; Vol. V. edd. G. Pertz, G. Waitz, H. Brunner, Hannoverae, 1835-1889.

Pallottini, S., *Collectio omnium conclusionum et resolutionum quae in causis propositis apud Sacram Congregationem Cardinalium S. Concilii Tridentini... Interpretum prodierunt ab eius institutione anno 1564 ad annum 1860, distinctis titulis alphabetico ordine per materias digesta,* 18 vols., Romae, 1868-1895.

Potthast, Augustus, *Regesta Pontificum Romanorum inde ab anno post Christum natum MCXCVIII ad annum MCCCIV,* 2 vols., Berolini, 1874-1875.

S. Romanae Rotae Decisiones seu Sententiae (ab anno 1909), Romae, Typis Vaticanis, 1912-

Schroeder, H. J., *Canons and Decrees of the Council of Trent: Original Text with English Translation,* St. Louis: Herder, 1941.

REFERENCE WORKS

Aertnys, J.-Damen, C. *Theologia Moralis,* 14. ed., 2 vols., Taurinorum Augustae: Marietti, 1944.

American Law and Procedure, A Systematic, Non-Technical Treatment of American Law and Procedure, 14 vols., Chicago: La Salle Extension University, 1944.

Augustine, Charles, *A Commentary on the New Code of Canon Law,* 8 vols., St. Louis: Herder, 1918-1922.

Aquinas, St. Thomas, *Summa Theologica,* 6 vols., Taurini: Marietti, 1932.

Ayrinhac, H. A.-Lydon, P. J., *Penal Legislation in the New Code of Canon Law,* New York: Benziger Brothers, Inc., 1936.

Barbosa, Augustinus, *Collectanea Doctorum tam Veterum quam Recentiorum in Ius Pontificium Universum,* 6 vols., in 3, Lugduni, 1716.

Bernardus Papiensis, *Summa Decretalium,* ed. E. A. Th. Laspeyres, Ratisbonae, 1860.

Berutti, P. C., *Institutiones Iuris Canonici,* 5 vols., Romae: Marietti, 1936-1943.

Beste, U., *Introductio in Codicem,* 2. ed., Collegeville, Minn.: St. John's Abbey Press, 1944.

Blat, A., *Commentarium Textus Codicis Iuris Canonici,* Liber V, *De Delictis et Poenis,* Romae: Collegio "Angelico," 1924.

Bouix, D., *De Judiciis Ecclesiasticis,* 2 vols., Parisiis, 1855.

Bourret, Francois, *Des Sentences Ecclésiastiques,* Montpellier, 1909.

Bouscaren, T. L.-Ellis, A. C., *Canon Law,* Milwaukee: The Bruce Publishing Co., 1946.

Cammeo, I., *Ordinamento Giuridico dello Stato della Città del Vaticano,* Firenze: Bemporad, 1932.

Catholic Encyclopedia, The, 15 vols., with index and 2 supplements, New York: 1907-1922.

Cavagnis, Felix, *Institutiones Iuris Publici Ecclesiastici,* Pars Secunda Specialis, 2. ed., Romae, 1889.

Chelodi, Ioannes,-Ciprotti, Pio, *De Delictis et Poenis,* 5. ed., Trento: Libraria Moderna Editrice, 1943.

Cicognani, Amleto, *Canon Law,* 2. rev. ed., authorized English version by J. O'Hara and F. Brennan, Westminster, Maryland: The Newman Bookship, 1946.

Clancy, Patrick, *The Local Religious Superior,* The Catholic University of America Canon Law Studies, n. 175, Washington, D. C.: The Catholic University of America Press, 1943.

Cocchi, G., *Commentarium in Codicem Iuris Canonici ad Usum Scholarum* 8 vols. Vol. VIII, 4. ed., Taurinorum Augustae; Casa Editrice Marietti, 1938.

Coronata, Matthaeus Conte (A), *Institutiones Iuris Canonici ad Usum Utriusque Cleri et Scholarum,* 2. ed., 5 vols., Taurini: Marietti, 1939-1947.

...*Manuale Practicum Iuris Disciplinaris et Criminalis Regularium,* Taurini: Marietti, 1938.

...*Pene e Sanzioni Canoniche Estragiudiziali,* Romae: L.I.C.E.-R. Berruti & C., 1933.

D'Annibale, J., *Summula Theologiae Moralis,* 2. ed., 3 vols., Romae, 1888-1892.

De Meester, A., *Juris Canonici et Juris Canonico-Civilis Compendium,* nova editio, 3 vols., in 4, Brugis: Desclee de Brouwer et Soc., 1921-1928.

De Luca, J. B., *Theatrum Veritatis et Iustitiae,* 5 vols., Venetiis, 1734.

Esswein, A. A., *Extrajudicial Coercive Powers of Ecclesiastical Superiors,* The Catholic University of America Canon Law Studies, n. 127, Washington, D. C.: The Catholic University of America Press, 1941.

Fagnanus, P., *Commentaria in Quinque Libros Decretalium,* 5 vols., Venetiis, 1709.

Fedele, Pio, *Discorso Generale sull' Ordinamento Canonico,* Padova: Cedam, 1941.

Feuerbach, P. A., *Lehrbuch des gemeinen in Deutschland geltenden peinlichen Privatrechts,* 14. ed. prepared by C. J. A. Mittermaier, Giessen: G. F. Heyer, 1847.

Ferraris, Lucius, *Prompta Bibliotheca, Canonica, Iuridica, Moralis, Theologica, necnon Ascetica, Polemica, Rubricistica, Historica,* 9 vols., Romae, 1885-1899.

Frison, Basil, *The Retroactivity of Law,* The Catholic University of America Canon Law Studies, No. 231, Washington, D. C.: The Catholic University of America Press, 1946.

Gonzalez-Tellez, Manuel, *Commentaria Perpetua in Quinque Libros Decretalium,* 5 vols. in 4, Venetiis, 1699.

Harper's Latin Dictionary, edited by E. A. Andrews, revised by Charlton T. Lewis and Charles Short, New York: American Book Co., 1907.

Hinschius, Paul, *Das Kirchenrecht der Katholiken und Protestanten in Deutschland,* 6 vols., Berlin, 1869-1897.

Hollweck, Joseph, *Die kirchlichen Strafgesetze,* Mainz, 1899.

Hostiensis, (Henricus de Segusio), *Summa Aurea,* Venetiis, 1570.

Ioannes Andreae, *In Sextum Decretalium Librum Novella Commentaria,* 5 vols., Venetiis, 1581.

Latini, J., *Summa Lineamenta Iuris Criminalis Philosophici,* Romae: Marietti, 1924.

Lauer, Arcturus, *Index Verborum Codicis Iuris Canonici,* Typis Polyglottis Vaticanis, 1941.

Lega, Michael, *Praelectiones in Textum Iuris Canonici, De Delictis et Poenis,* ed. altera, Romae 1910.

Maroto, P., *Institutiones Iuris Canonici ad Normam Novi Codicis,* 2 vols., Madrid, 1919.

Maschat, R., *Institutiones Canonicae,* ed. ab Ubaldo Giraldi a S. Cajetano, 4 vols. in 2, Florentiae, 1854.

Merkelbach, B. H., *Summa Theologiae Moralis,* 3. ed., 3 vols., Parisiis: Desclée, 1939.

Michiels, Gommarus, *Normae Generales Iuris Canonici,* 2 vols., Lublin-Polonia: Universitas Catholica, 1929.

...*De Delictis et Poenis,* Vol. I, Lublin-Polonia: Universitas Catholica, 1934.

Migne, J. P. *Patrologiae Cursus Completus, Series Latina,* 221 vols., Parisiis, 1844-1855.

Mourret, F.-Thompson, N., *A History of the Catholic Church,* 6 vols., St. Louis: Herder Book Co., 1931-1946.

Muñiz, T., *Procedimientos Eclesiásticos,* 2. ed., 3 vols., Sevilla, 1925.

Murphy, E. J. *Suspension ex Informata Conscientia,* The Catholic University of America Canon Law Studies, No. 76, Washington, D. C.: The Catholic University of America, 1932.

Noldin, H.-Schmitt, A., *Summa Theologiae Moralis,* 24. ed., 3 vols., Romae: Pustet, 1936.

Ottaviani, A., *Compendium Iuris Publici Ecclesiastici,* Typis Polyglottis Vaticanis, 1936.

Pallottini, S., *Pugna Iuris Pontifiicii Statuentis Suspensiones extraiudicialiter seu ex Informata Conscientia, et Imperii Easdem Obrogare Molientis,* Viennae, 1863.

Panormitanus, Abbas (Nicolaus de Tudeschis), *Omnia Quae Extant Commentaria in Decretales,* 6 vols., Venetiis, 1588.

Peckius, Petrus, *Opera Omnia,* Antverpiae, 1666.

Phillips, Georgius, *Compendium Iuris Ecclesiastici,* auctum et emendatum ed. F. H. Vering, 3. ed., Latinae versionis prima, Ratisbonae, 1875.

Pirhing, Ernricus, *Ius Canonicum Nova Methodo Explicatum,* 5 vols., Dilingae, 1674-1678.

Rainer, E. G., *Suspension of Clerics,* The Catholic University of America Canon Law Ctudies, N. 111, Washington, D. C.: The Catholic University of America, 1937.

Reiffenstuel, Anacletus, *Ius Canonicum Universum,* 7 vols., Parisiis, 1864-1870.

Ried-Brig, (A) Th., *Manuale Practicum Iuris Disciplinaris et Criminalis,* Romae, Typis Vaticanis, 1902.

Roberti, F., *De Delictis et Poenis,* 2 vols., Romae: Pontificium Institutum Utriusque Iuris, 1930-1938.

Salucci, R., *Il Diritto Penale,* 2 vols., Subiaco, 1926-1930.

Schmalzgrueber, Franciscus, *Ius Ecclesiasticum Universum,* 5 vols. in 12, Romae, 1843-1845.

Schroeder, H. J., *Disciplinary Decrees of the General Councils: Text, Translation, and Commentary,* St. Louis: Herder, 1937.

Seagle, W., *The Quest for Law,* New York: Alfred Knopf, 1941.

Smith, S. B. *Elements of Ecclesiastical Law,* 3 vols., Vol. III, *Ecclesiastical Punishments,* New York: Benziger Bros., 1888.

Sole, J., *De Delictis et Poenis,* Romae: Pustet, 1920.

Studi in Onore di Francesco Scaduto, 2 vols. Firenze: Polygrafica Universitaria, 1936.

Suarez, Franciscus, *Opera Omnia,* ed. nova, 28 vols., Vol. V., *Tractatus de Legibus et Legislatore Deo,* Parisiis, 1856.

Tarquini, C., *Iuris Ecclesiastici Institutiones,* 4. ed., Romae, 1875.

Van Hove, A., *Commentarium Lovaniense in Codicem Iuris Canonici,* 1 vol. in 5 toms., Tom. I, *Prolegomena,* 2. ed., Mechliniae: H. Dessain, 1945; Tom. II, *De Legibus Ecclesiasticis,* Mechliniae-Romae: H. Dessain, 1930.

Vermeersch, A.-Creusen, J., *Epitome Iuris Canonici,* 3 vols., Vol. III, 5. ed., Mechliniae: Dessain, 1936.

Wernz, F. X., *Ius Decretalium,* 6 vols., Romae, 1898-1905.

Wernz, F. X.-Vidal, P., *Ius Canonicum,* 7 vols. in 8, Romae: Apud Aedes Universitatis Gregorianae, 1923-1938. Vol. I, *Normae generalis,* 1938; Vol. VI, *De Processibus,* 1927; Vol. VII, *Ius Poenale Ecclesiasticum,* 1937.

ARTICLES

Bartoccetti, V., "De Iure et Officio Promotoris Iustitiae Accusandi Matrimonium," *Apollinaris,* X (1937), 570-588.

Cappello, F., "Irrogatio Poenae per Modum Praecepti extra Iudicium," *Periodica,* XIX (1930), 36-38.

Coronata, Matthaeus Conte (A), "Pene e procedimenti 'ad modum praecepti'," *Perfice Munus,* VII (1932), 34-38; 121-128; 192-200; 270-273; 352-356.

D'Angelo, S., "Nozione del Delitto nel Codice di Diritto Canonico," *ETL,* III (1926), 210-218.

Giacchi, Orio, "Precedenti Canonistici del Principio 'Nullum Crimen sine Praevia Lege Poenali'," *Studi in Onore di Francesco Scaduto,* Vol. I, 435-449.

Noval, J., "De ratione corrigendi ac puniendi sive in iudicio sive extra iure Codicis J. C.," *Jus Pont.,* I-II (1921-1922), 147-156; III (1923), 36-40, 204-210.

Petrani, A., "De S. C. pro Ecclesia Orientali," *Apollinaris,* X (1937), 28-46.

Roberti, F., "Respectus Sociales in Codice Iuris Canonici," *Apollinaris,* X (1937), 342-394.

Van Hove, A., "Leges Quae Ordini Publico Consulunt," *ETL,* I (1924), 153-167.

Vidal, P., "Notio Delicti in Iure Codicis," *Jus Pont.,* (1921), 99-102.

PERIODICALS

Apollinaris, Romae, 1928-

Ephemerides Theologicae Lovanienses, Lovanii, 1924-

Jus Pontificum, Romae, 1921-1940.

Perfice Munus, Torino, 1926-

Periodica de Re Canonica et Morali utili Praesertim Religiosis et Missionariis, Brugis, 1905-

ABBREVIATIONS

AAS—*Acta Apostolicae Sedis.*

ASS—*Acta Sanctae Sedis.*

Bruns—*Canones Apostolorum et Conciliorum Saeculorum IV-VII.*

Collectanea—*Collectanea S. Congregationis de Propaganda Fide.*

Commentaria—Panormitanus, *Omnia Quae Extant Commentaria in Decretales.*

CSEL—*Corpus Scriptorum Ecclesiasticorum Latinorum.*

Decisiones—*S. Romanae Rotae Decisiones seu Sententiae.*

Epitome—Vermeersch-Creusen, *Epitome Iuris Canonici.*

ETL—*Ephemerides Theologicae Lovanienses,* Lovanii.

Fontes—*Codicis Iuris Canonici Fontes,* cura... Gasparri editi.

Hardouin—*Acta Conciliorum etc.*

Institutiones—Coronata, *Institutiones Iuris Canonici.*

Ius Canonicum—Pirhing, *Ius Canonicum Nova Methodo Explicatum.*

Jaffé—*Regesta Pontificum Romanorum, etc.*

Jus Pont.—*Jus Pontificium.*

Kirchenrecht—Hinschius, *Das Kirchenrecht der Katholiken und Protestanten in Deutschland.*

Mansi—*Sacrorum Conciliorum Nova et Amplissima Collectio.*

MGH—*Monumenta Germaniae Historica.*

MPL—Migne, *Patrologiae Cursus Completus, Series Latina.*

Potthast—*Regesta Pontificum Romanorum, etc.*

ALPHABETICAL INDEX

BIOGRAPHICAL NOTE

James Vincent Casey was born on September 22, 1914, at Osage, Iowa. He received his elementary and high school education in the public schools of that city. In 1936 he was graduated from Loras College of Dubuque, Iowa, with the degree of Bachelor of Arts. In the fall of that year he entered the North American College in Rome, and was enrolled at the Gregorian University for his theological studies. After his ordination to the priesthood on the feast of the Immaculate Conception, December 8, 1939, he returned to this country and became engaged in parochial duties. During the war, he was commissioned and served as a Chaplain in the United States Navy. Upon his discharge from naval service, he entered the School of Canon Law at the Catholic University of America in the fall of 1946; he received the degree of Bachelor in Canon Law in June, 1947, and the degree of Licentiate in Canon Law in June, 1948.

CANON LAW STUDIES*

1. Freriks, Rev. Celestine A., C.PP.S., J.C.D., Religious Congregations in Their External Relations, 121 pp., 1916.

2. Galliher, Rev. Daniel M., O.P., J.C.D., Canonical Elections, 117 pp., 1917.

3. Borkowski, Rev. Aurelius L., O.F.M., J.C.D., De Confraternitatibus Ecclesiasticis, 136 pp., 1918.

4. Castillo, Rev. Cayo, J.C.D., Disertación Histórico-Canónica sobre la Potestad del Cabildo en Sede Vacante o Impedida del Vicario Capitular, 99 pp., 1919 (1918).

5. Kubelbeck, Rev. William J., S.T.B., J.C.D., The Sacred Penitentiaria and Its Relation to Faculties of Ordinaries and Priests, 129 pp., 1918.

6. Petrovits, Rev. Joseph, J.C., S.T.D., J.C.D., The New Church Law on Matrimony, X-461 pp., 1919.

7. Hickey, Rev. John J., S.T.B., J.C.D., Irregularities and Simple Impediments in the New Code of Canon Law, 100 pp., 1920.

8. Klekotka, Rev. Peter J., S.T.B., J.C.D., Diocesan Consultors, 179 pp., 1920.

9. Wanenmacher, Rev. Francis, J.C.D., The Evidence in Ecclesiastical Procedure Affecting the Marriage Bond, 1920 (Printed 1935).

10. Golden, Rev. Henry Francis, J.C.D., Parochial Benefices in the New Code, IV-119 pp., 1921 (Printed 1925).

11. Koudelka, Rev. Charles J., J.C.D., Pastors, Their Rights and Duties According to the New Code of Canon Law, 211 pp., 1921.

12. Melo, Rev. Antonius, O.F.M., J.C.D., De Exemptione Regularium, X-188 pp., 1921.

13. Schaaf, Rev. Valentine Theodore, O.F.M., S.T.B., J.C.D., The Cloister, X-180 pp., 1921.

14. Burke, Rev. Thomas Joseph, S.T.D., J.C.D., Competence in Ecclesiastical Tribunals, IV-117 pp., 1922.

15. Leech, Rev. George Leo, J.C.D., A Comparative Study of the Constitution "Apostolicae Sedis" and the "Codex Juris Canonici," 179 pp., 1922.

16. Motry, Rev. Hubert Louis, S.T.D., J.C.D., Diocesan Faculties According to the Code of Canon Law, II-167 pp., 1922.

*—All published numbers of this series are available from the Catholic University of America Press, 620 Michigan Ave., N.E., Washington 17, D. C., except the following: nn. 1-114 inclusive, 116, 118, 120, 121, 122, 123, 136, 153, 162, 182 and 198. But the following numbers, recently reissued, are obtainable from The Jurist, The Catholic University of America, Washington 17, D. C., namely: Numbers 5, 7, 11, 17, 18, 19, 26, 28, 30, 31, 34, 42, 44, 51, 52 and 61.

17. Murphy, Rev. George Lawrence, J.C.D., Delinquencies and Penalties in the Administration and the Reception of the Sacraments, IV-121 pp., 1924.

18. O'Reilly, Rev. John Anthony, S.T.B., J.C.D., Ecclesiastical Sepulture in the New Code of Canon Law, II-129 pp., 1923.

19. Michalicka, Rev. Wenceslas Cyrill, O.S.B., J.C.D., Judicial Procedure in Dismissal of Clerical Exempt Religious, 107 pp., 1923.

20. Dargin, Rev. Edward Vincent, S.T.B., J.C.D., Reserved Cases According to the Code of Canon Law, IV-103 pp., 1924.

21. Godfrey, Rev. John A., S.T.B., J.C.D., The Right of Patronage According to the Code of Canon Law, 153 pp., 1924.

22. Hagedorn, Rev. Francis Edward, J.C.D., General Legislation on Indulgences, II-154 pp., 1924.

23. King, Rev. James Ignatius, J.C.D., The Administration of the Sacraments to Dying Non-Catholics, V-141 pp., 1924.

24. Winslow, Rev. Francis Joseph, O.F.M., J.C.D., Vicars and Prefects Apostolic, IV-149 pp., 1924.

25. Correa, Rev. Jose Servelion, S.T.L., J.C.D., La Potestad Legislativa de la Iglesia Católica, IV-127 pp., 1925.

26. Dugan, Rev. Henry Francis, A.M., J.C.D., The Judiciary Department of the Diocesan Curia, 87 pp., 1925.

27. Keller, Rev. Charles Frederick, S.T.B., J.C.D., Mass Stipends, 167 pp., 1925.

28. Paschang, Rev. John Linus, J.C.D., The Sacramentals According to the Code of Canon Law, 129 pp., 1925.

29. Piontek, Rev. Cyrillus, O.F.M., S.T.B., J.C.D., De Indulto Exclaustrationis necnon Saecularizationis, XIII-289 pp., 1925.

30. Kearney, Rev. Richard Joseph, S.T.B., J.C.D., Sponsors at Baptism According to the Code of Canon Law, IV-127 pp., 1925.

31. Bartlett, Rev. Chester Joseph, A.M., LL.B., J.C.D., The Tenure of Parochial Property in the United States of America, V-108 pp., 1926.

32. Kilker, Rev. Adrian Jerome, J.C.D., Extreme Unction, V-4125 pp., 1926.

33. McCormick, Rev. Robert Emmett, J.C.D., Confessors of Religious VIII-266 pp., 1926.

34. Miller, Rev. Newton Thomas, J.C.D., Founded Masses According to the Code of Canon Law, VII-93 pp., 1926.

35. Roelker, Rev. Edward G., S.T.D., J.C.D., Principles of Privilege According to the Code of Canon Law, XI-166 pp., 1926.

36. Bakalarczyk, Rev. Richards, M.I.C., J.U.D., De Novitiatu, VIII-208 pp., 1927.

37. Pizzuti, Rev. Lawrence, O.F.M., J.U.L., De Parochis Religiosis, 1927. (Not Printed.)

38. Bliley, Rev. Nicholas Martin, O.S.B., J.C.D., Altars According to the Code of Canon Law, XIX-132 pp., 1927.

39. Brown, Mr. Brendan Francis, A.B., LL.M., J.U.D., The Canonical Juristic Personality with Special Reference to its Status in the United States of America, V-212 pp., 1927.

40. Cavanaugh, Rev. William Thomas, C.P., J.U.D., The Reservation of the Blessed Sacrament, VIII-101 pp., 1927.

41. Doheny, Rev. William J., C.S.C., A.B., J.C.D., Church Property: Modes of Acquisition, X-118 pp., 1927.

42. Feldhaus, Rev. Aloysius H., C.PP.S., J.C.D., Oratories, IX-141 pp., 1927.

43. Kelly, Rev. James Patrick, A.B., J.C.D., The Jurisdiction of the Simple Confessor, X-208 pp., 1927.

44. Neuberger, Rev. Nicholas J., J.C.D., Canon 6 or the Relation of the Codex Juris Canonici to the Preceding Legislation, V-95 pp., 1927.

45. O'Keefe, Rev. Gerald Michael, J.C.D., Matrimonial Dispensations, Powers of Bishops, Priests, and Confessors, VIII-232 pp., 1927.

46. Quigley, Rev. Joseph A. M., A.B., J.C.D., Condemned Societies, 139 pp., 1927.

47. Zaplotnik, Rev. Johannes Leo, J.C.D., De Vicariis Foraneis, X-142 pp., 1927.

48. Duskie, Rev. John Aloysius, A.B., J.C.D., The Canonical Status of the Orientals in the United States, VIII-196 pp., 1928.

49. Hyland, Rev. Francis Edward, J.C.D., Excommunication, Its Nature, Historical Development and Effects, VIII-181 pp., 1928.

50. Reinmann, Rev. Gerald Joseph, O.M.C., J.C.D., The Third Order Secular of Saint Francis, 201 pp., 1928.

51. Schenk, Rev. Francis J., J.C.D., The Matrimonial Impediments of Mixed Religion and Disparity of Cult, XVI-318 pp., 1929.

52. Coady, Rev. John Joseph, S.T.D., J.U.D., A.M., The Appointment of Pastors, VIII-150 pp., 1929.

53. Kay, Rev. Thomas Henry, J.C.D., Competence in Matrimonial Procedure, VIII-164 pp., 1929.

54. Turner, Rev. Sidney Joseph, C.P., J.U.D., The Vow of Poverty, XLIX-217 pp., 1929.

55. Kearney, Rev. Raymond A., A.B., S.T.D., J.C.D., The Principles of Delegation, VII-149 pp., 1929.

56. Conran, Rev. Edward James, A.B., J.C.D., The Interdict, V-163 pp., 1930.

57. O'Neill, Rev. William H., J.C.D., Papal Rescripts of Favor, VII-218 pp., 1930.

58. Bastnagel, Rev. Clement Vincent, J.U.D., The Appointment of Parochial Adjutants and Assistants, XV-257 pp., 1930.

59. Ferry, Rev. William A., A.B., J.C.D., Stole Fees, V-136 pp., 1930.

60. Costello, Rev. John Michael, A.B., J.C.D., Domicile and Quasi-Domicile, VII-201 pp., 1930.

61. Kremer, Rev. Michael Nicholas, A.B., S.T.B., J.C.D., Church Support in the United States, VI-136 pp., 1930.

62. Angulo, Rev. Luis, C.M., J.C.D., Legislación de la Iglesia sobre la intención en la applicación de la Santa Misa, VII-104 pp., 1931.

63. Frey, Rev. Wolfgang Norbert, O.S.B., A.B., J.C.D., The Act of Religious Profession, VIII-174 pp., 1931.

64. Roberts, Rev. James Brendan, A.B., J.C.D., The Banns of Marriage, XIV-140 pp., 1931.

65. Ryder, Rev. Raymond Aloysius, A.B., J.C.D., Simony, IX-151 pp., 1931.

66. Campagna, Rev. Angelo, Ph.D., J.U.D., Il Vicario Generale del Vescovo, VII-205 pp., 1931.

67. Cox, Rev. Joseph Godfrey, A.B., J.C.D., The Administration of Seminaries, VI-124 pp., 1931.

68. Gregory, Rev. Donald J., J.U.D., The Pauline Privilege, XV-165 pp., 1931.

69 Donohue, Rev. John F., J.C.D., The Impediment of Crime, VII-110 pp., 1931.

70. Dooley, Rev. Eugene A., O.M.I., J.C.D., Church Law on Sacred Relics, IX-143 pp., 1931.

71. Orth, Rev. Clement Raymond, O.M.C., J.C.D., The Approbation of Religious Institutes, 171 pp., 1931.

72. Pernicone, Rev. Joseph M., A.B. J.C.D., The Ecclesiastical Prohibition of Books, XII-267 pp., 1932.

73. Clinton, Rev. Connell, A.B., J.C.D., The Paschal Precept, IX-108 pp., 1932.

74. Donnelly, Rev. Francis B., A.M., S.T.L., J.C.D., The Diocesan Synod, VIII-125 pp., 1932.

75. Torrente, Rev. Camilo, C.M.F., J.C.D., Las Procesiones Sagradas, V-145 pp., 1932.

76. Murphy, Rev. Edwin J., C.PP.S., J.C.D., Suspension Ex Informata Conscientia, XI-122 pp., 1932.

77. MacKenzie, Rev. Eric F., A.M., S.T.L., J.C.D., The Delict of Heresy in its Commission, Penalization, Absolution, VII-124 pp., 1932.

78. Lyons, Rev. Avitus E., S.T.B., J.C.D., The Collegiate Tribunal of First Instance, XI-147 pp., 1932.

79. Connolly, Rev. Thomas A., J.C.D., Appeals, XI-195, pp., 1932.

80. Sangmeister, Rev. Joseph V., A.B., J.C.D., Force and Fear as Precluding Matrimonial Consent, V-211 pp., 1932.

81. Jaeger, Rev. Leo A., A.B., J.C.D., The Administration of Vacant and Quasi-Vacant Episcopal Sees in the United States, IX-229 pp., 1932.

82. Rimlinger, Rev. Herbert T., J.C.D., Error Invalidating Matrimonial Consent, VII-79 pp., 1932.

83. BARRETT, REV. JOHN D. M., S.S., J.C.D., A Comparative Study of the Councils of Baltimore and the Code of Canon Law, IX-223 pp., 1932.

84. CARBERRY, REV. JOHN J., PH.D., S.T.D., J.C.D., The Juridical Form of Marriage, X-177 pp., 1934.

85. DOLAN, REV. JOHN L., A.B., J.C.D., The Defensor Vinculi, XII-157 pp., 1934.

86. HANNAN, REV. JEROME D., A.M., S.T.D., LL.B., J.C.D., The Canon Law of Wills, IX-517 pp., 1934.

87. LEMIEUX, REV. DELISE A., A.M., J.C.D., The Sentence in Ecclesiastical Procedure, IX-131 pp., 1934.

88. O'ROURKE, REV. JAMES J., A.B., J.C.D., Parish Registers, VII-109 pp., 1934.

89. TIMLIN, REV. BARTHOLOMEW, O.F.M., A.M., J.C.D., Conditional Matrimonial Consent, X-381 pp., 1934.

90. WAHL, REV. FRANCIS X., A.B., J.C.D., The Matrimonial Impediments of Consanguinity and Affinity, VI-125 pp., 1934.

91. WHITE, REV. ROBERT J., A.B., LL.B., S.T.B., J.C.D., Canonical Ante-Nuptial Promises and the Civil Law, VI-152 pp., 1934.

92. HERRERA, REV. ANTONIO PARRA, O.C.D., J.C.D., Legislación Ecclesiástica sobre el Ayuno y la Abstinencia, XI-191 pp., 1935.

93. KENNEDY, REV. EDWIN J., J.C.D., The Special Matrimonial Process in Cases of Evident Nullity, X-165 pp., 1935.

94. MANNING, REV. JOHN J., A.B., J.C.D., Presumption of Law in Matrimonial Procedure, XI-111 pp., 1935.

95. MOEDER, REV. JOHN M., J.C.D., The Proper Bishop for Ordination and Dimissorial Letters, VII-135 pp., 1935.

96. O'MARA, REV. WILLIAM A., A.B., J.C.D., Canonical Causes for Matrimonial Dispensations, IX-155 pp., 1935.

97. REILLY, REV. PETER, J.C.D., Residence of Pastors, IX-81 pp., 1935.

98. SMITH, REV. MARINER T., O.P., S.T.Lr., J.C.D., The Penal Law for Religious, VIII-169 pp., 1935.

99. WHALEN, REV. DONALD W., A.M., J.C.D., The Value of Testimonial Evidence in Matrimonial Procedure, XIII-297 pp., 1935.

100. CLEARY, REV. JOSEPH F., J.C.D., Canonical Limitations on the Alienation of Church Property, VIII-141 pp., 1936.

101. GLYNN, REV. JOHN C., J.C.D., The Promoter of Justice, XX-337 pp., 1936.

102. BRENNAN, REV. JAMES H., S.S., M.A., S.T.B., J.C.D., The Simple Convalidation of Marriage, VI-135 pp., 1937.

103. BRUNINI, REV. JOSEPH BERNARD, J.C.D., The Clerical Obligations of Canons 139 and 142, X-121 pp., 1937.

104. CONNOR, REV. MAURICE, A.B., J.C.D., The Administrative Removal of Pastors, VIII-159 pp., 1937.

105. GUILFOYLE, REV. MERLIN JOSEPH, J.C.D., Custom, XI-144 pp., 1937.

106. Hughes, Rev. James Austin, A.B., A.M., J.C.D., Witnesses in Criminal Trials of Clerics, IX-140 pp., 1937.

107. Jansen, Rev. Raymond J., A.B., S.T.L., J.C.D., Canonical Provisions for Catechetical Instruction, VII-153 pp., 1937.

108. Kealy, Rev. John James, A.B., J.C.D., The Introductory Libellus in Church Court Procedure, XI-121 pp., 1937.

109. McManus, Rev. James Edward, C.SS.R., J.C.D., The Administration of Temporal Goods in Religious Institutes, XVI-196 pp., 1937.

110. Moriarity, Rev. Eugene James, J.C.D., Oaths in Ecclesiastical Courts, X-115 pp., 1937.

111. Rainer, Rev. Eligius George, C.SS.R., J.C.D., Suspension of Clerics, XVII-249 pp., 1937.

112. Reilly, Rev. Thomas F., C.SS.R., J.C.D., Visitation of Religious, VI-95 pp., 1938.

113. Moriarity, Rev. Francis E., C.SS.R., J.C.D., The Extraordinary Absolution from Censures, XV-334 pp., 1938.

114. Connolly, Rev. Nicholas P., J.C.D., The Canonical Erection of Parishes, X-132 pp., 1938.

115. Donovan, Rev. James Joseph, J.C.D., The Pastor's Obligation in Prenuptial Investigation, XII-322 pp., 1938.

116. Harrigan, Rev. Robert J., M.A., S.T.B., J.C.D., The Radical Sanation of Invalid Marriages, VIII-208 pp., 1938.

117. Boffa, Rev. Conrad Humbert, J.C.D., Canonical Provisions for Catholic Schools, VII-211 pp., 1939.

118. Parsons, Rev. Anscar John, O.M.Cap., J.C.D., Canonical Elections, XII-236 pp., 1939.

119. Reilly, Rev. Edward Michael, A.B., J.C.D., The General Norms of Dispensation, XII-156 pp., 1939.

120. Ryan, Rev. Gerald Aloysius, A.B., J.C.D., Principles of Episcopal Jurisdiction, XII-172 pp., 1939.

121. Burton, Rev. Francis James, C.S.C., A.B., J.C.D., A Commentary on Canon 1125, X-222 pp., 1940.

122. Miaskiewicz, Rev. Francis Sigismund, J.C.D., Supplied Jurisdiction According to Canon 209, XII-340 pp., 1940.

123. Rice, Rev. Patrick William, A.B., J.C.D., Proof of Death in Prenuptial Investigation, VIII-156 pp., 1940.

124. Anglin, Rev. Thomas Francis, M.S., J.C.D., The Eucharistic Fast, VIII-183 pp., 1941.

125. Coleman, Rev. John Jerome, J.C.D., The Minister of Confirmation, VI-153 pp., 1941.

126. Downs, Rev. John Emmanuel, A.B., J.C.D., The Concept of Clerical Immunity, XI-163 pp., 1941.

127. Esswein, Rev. Anthony Albert, J.C.D., Extrajudicial Penal Powers of Ecclesiastical Superiors, X-144 pp., 1941.

128. FARRELL, REV. BENJAMIN FRANCIS, M.A., S.T.L., J.C.D., The Rights and Duties of the Local Ordinary Regarding Congregations of Women Religious of Pontifical Approval, V-195 pp., 1941.

129. FEENEY, REV. THOMAS JOHN, A.B., S.T.L., J.C.D., Restitutio in Integrum VI-169 pp., 1941.

130. FINDLAY, REV. STEPHEN WILLIAM, O.S.B., A.B., J.C.D., Canonical Norms Governing the Deposition and Degradation of Clerics, XVII-279 pp., 1941.

131. GOODWINE, REV. JOHN, A.B., S.T.L., J.C.D., The Right of the Church to Acquire Property, VIII-119 pp., 1941.

132. HESTON, REV. EDWARD LOUIS, C.S.C., Ph.D., S.T.D., J.C.D., The Alienation of Church Property in the United States, XII-222 pp., 1941.

133. HOGAN, REV. JAMES JOHN, A.B., S.T.L., J.C.D., Judicial Advocates and Procurators, XIII-200 pp., 1941.

134. KEALY, REV. THOMAS M., A.B., Litt.B., J.C.D., Dowry of Women Religious, IX-152 pp., 1941.

135. KEENE, REV. MICHAEL JAMES, O.S.B., J.C.D., Religious Ordinaries and Canon 198, V-164 pp., 1942.

136. KERIN, REV. CHARLES A., S.S., M.A., S.T.B., J.C.D., The Privation of Christian Burial, XVI-279 pp., 1941.

137. LOUIS, REV. WILLIAM FRANCIS, M.A., J.C.D., Diocesan Archives, X-101 pp., 1941.

138. MCDEVITT, REV. GILBERT JOSEPH, A.B., J.C.D., Legitimacy and Legitimation, X-247 pp., 1941.

139. MCDONOUGH, REV. THOMAS JOSEPH, A.B., J.C.D., Apostolic Administrators, X-217 pp., 1941.

140. MEIER, REV. CARL ANTHONY, A.B., J.C.D., Penal Administrative Procedure Against Negligent Pastors, XI-240 pp., 1941.

141. SCHMIDT, REV. JOHN ROGG, A.B., J.C.D., The Principles of Authentic Interpretation in Canon 17 of the Code of Canon Law, XII-331 pp., 1941

142. SLAFKOSKY, REV. ANDREW LEONARD, A.B., J.C.D., The Canonical Episcopal Visitation of the Diocese, X-197 pp., 1941.

143, SWOBODA, REV. INNOCENT ROBERT, O.F.M., J.C.D., Ignorance in Relation to the Imputability of Delicts, IX-271 pp., 1941.

144. DUBE, REV. ARTHUR JOSEPH, A.B., J.C.D., The General Principles for the Reckoning of Time in Canon Law, VIII-299 pp., 1941.

145. MCBRIDE, REV. JAMES T., A.B., J.C.D., Incardination and Excardination of Seculars, XX-585 pp., 1941.

146. KRÓL, REV. JOHN T., J.C.D., The Defendant in Ecclesiastical Trials, XII-207 pp., 1942.

147. COMYNS, REV. JOSEPH J., C.SS.R., A.B., J.C.D., Papal and Episcopal Administration of Church Property, XIV-155 pp., 1942.

148. Barry, Rev. Garrett Francis, O.M.I., J.C.D., Violation of the Cloister XII-260 pp., 1942.

149. Bolduc, Rev. Gatien, C.S.V., A.B., S.T.L., J.C.D., Les Études dans les Religions Cléricales, VIII-155 pp., 1942.

150. Boyle, Rev. David John, M.A., J.C.D., The Juridic Effects of Moral Certitude on Pre-Nuptial Guarantees, XII-188 pp., 1942.

151. Canavan, Rev. Walter Joseph, M.A., Litt.D., J.C.D., The Profession of Faith, XII-143 pp., 1942.

152. Desrochers, Rev. Bruno, A.B., Ph.L., S.T.B., J.C.D., Le Premier Concile Plénier de Québec et le Code de Droit Canonique, XIV-186 pp., 1942.

153. Dillon, Rev. Robert Edward, A.B., J.C.D., Common Law Marriage, X-148 pp., 1942.

154. Dodwell, Rev. Edward John, Ph.D., S.T.B., J.C.D., The Time and Place for the Celebration of Marriage, X-156 pp., 1942.

155. Donnellan, Rev. Thomas Andrew, A.B., J.C.D., The Obligation of the Missa pro Populo, VII-131 pp., 1942.

156. Eltz, Rev. Louis Anthony, A.B., J.C.D., Cooperation in Crime, XII-208 pp., 1942.

157. Gass, Rev. Sylvester Francis, M.A., J.C.D., Ecclesiastical Pensions, XI-206 pp., 1942.

158. Guiniven, Rev. John Joseph, C.SS.R., J.C.D., The Precept of Hearing Mass, XIV-188 pp., 1942.

159. Gulczynski, Rev. John Theophilus, J.C.D., The Desecration and Violation of Churches, X-126 pp., 1942.

160. Hammill, Rev. John Leo, M.A., J.C.D., The Obligations of the Traveler According to Canon 14, VIII-204 pp., 1942.

161. Haydt, Rev. John Joseph, A.B., J.C.D., Reserved Benefices, XI-148 pp., 1942.

162. Huser, Rev. Roger John, O.F.M., A.B., J.C.D., The Crime of Abortion in Canon Law, XII-187 pp., 1942.

163. Kearney, Rev. Francis Patrick, A.B., S.T.L., J.C.D., The Principles of Canon 1127, X-162 pp., 1942.

164. Linahen, Rev. Leo James, S.T.L., JC.D., De Absolutione Complicis in Peccato Turpi, V-114 pp., 1942.

165. McCloskey, Rev. Joseph Aloysius, A.B., J.C.D., The Subject of Ecclesiastical Law According to Canon 12, XVII-246 pp., 1942.

166. O'Neill, Rev. Francis Joseph, C.SS.R., J.C.D., The Dismissal of Religious in Temporary Vows, XIII-220 pp., 1942.

167. Prince, Rev. John Edward, A.B., S.T.B., J.C.D., The Diocesan Chancellor, X-136 pp., 1942.

168. Riesner, Rev. Albert Joseph, C.SS.R., J.C.D., Apostates and Fugitives from Religious Institutes, IX-168 pp., 1942.

169. STENGER, REV. JOSEPH BERNARD, J.C.D., The Mortgaging of Church Property, 186 pp., 1942.

170. WALDRON, REV. JOSEPH FRANCIS, A.B., J.C.D., The Minister of Baptism, XII-197 pp., 1942.

171. WILLETT, REV. ROBERT ALBERT, J.C.D., The Probative Value of Documents in Ecclesiastical Trials, X-124 pp., 1942.

172. WOEBER, REV. EDWARD MARTIN, M.A., J.C.D., The Interpellations, XII-161 pp., 1942.

173. BENKO, REV. MATTHEW ALOYSIUS, O.S.B., M.A., J.C.D., The Abbot *Nullius*, XVI-148 pp., 1943.

174. CHRIST, REV. JOSEPH JAMES, M.A., S.T.L., J.C.D., Dispensation from Vindicative Penalties, XIV-285 pp., 1943.

175. CLANCY, REV. PATRICK M. J., O.P., A.B., S.T.Lr., J.C.D., The Local Religious Superior, X-229 pp., 1943.

176. CLARKE, REV. THOMAS JAMES, J.C.D., Parish Societies, XII-147 pp., 1943.

177. CONNOLLY, REV. JOHN PATRICK, S.T.L., J.C.D., Synodal Examiners and Parish Priest Consultors, X-223 pp., 1943.

178. DRUMM, REV. WILLIAM MARTIN, A.B., J.C.D., Hospital Chaplains, XII-175 pp., 1943.

179. FLANAGAN, REV. BERNARD JOSEPH, A.B., S.T.L., J.C.D., The Canonical Erection of Religious Houses, X-147 pp., 1943.

180. KELLEHER, REV. STEPHEN, A.B., S.T.B., J.C.D., Discussions with Non-Catholics: Canonical Legislation, X-93 pp., 1943.

181. LEWIS, REV. GORDIAN, C.P., J.C.D., Chapters in Religious Institutes, XII-169 pp., 1943.

182. MARX, REV. ADOLPH, J.C.D., The Declaration of Nullity of Marriages Contracted Outside the Church, X-151 pp., 1943.

183. MATULENAS, REV. RAYMOND ANTHONY, O.S.B., A.B., J.C.D., Communication, a Source of Privileges, XII-225 pp., 1943.

184. O'LEARY, REV. CHARLES GERARD, C.SS.R., J.C.D., Religious Dismissed After Perpetual Profession, X-213 pp., 1943.

185. POWER, REV. CORNELIUS MICHAEL, J.C.D., The Blessing of Cemeteries, XII-231 pp., 1943.

186. SHUHLER, REV. RALPH VINCENT, O.S.A., J.C.D., Privileges of Religious to Absolve and Dispense, XII-195 pp., 1943.

187. ZIOLKOWSKI, REV. THADDEUS STANISLAUS, A.B., J.C.D., The Consecration and Blessing of Churches, XII-151 pp., 1943.

188. HENEGHAN, REV. JOHN JOSEPH, S.T.D., J.C.D., The Marriages of Unworthy Catholics: Canons 1065 and 1066, XVI-213 pp., 1944.

189. CARROLL, REV. COLEMAN FRANCIS, M.A., S.T.L., J.C.L., Charitable Institutions.

190. CIESLUK, REV. JOSEPH EDWARD, PH.B., S.T.L., J.C.D., National Parishes in the United States, VI-178 pp., 1944.

191. Coburn, Rev. Vincent Paul, A.B., J.C.D., Marriages of Conscience, XII-172 pp., 1944.

192. Connors, Rev. Charles Paul, C.S.Sp., A.B., J.C.D., Extra-Judicial Procurators in the Code of Canon Law, X-94 pp., 1944.

193. Coyle, Rev. Paul Raymond, A.B., J.C.D., Judicial Exceptions, X-142 pp., 1944.

194. Fair, Rev. Bartholomew Francis, A.B., S.T.L., J.C.D., The Impediment of Abduction, XII-122 pp., 1944.

195. Gallagher, Rev. Thomas Raphael, O.P., A.B., S.T.L8., J.C.D., The Examination of the Qualities of the Ordinand, X-166 pp., 1944.

196. Gannon, Rev. John Mark, S.T.L., J.C.D., The Interstices Required for the Promotion to Orders, XII-100 pp., 1944.

197. Goldsmith, Rev. J. William, B.C.S., S.T.L., J.C.D., The Competence of Church and State Over Marriages—Disputed Points, X-128 pp., 1944.

198. Goodwine, Rev. Joseph Gerard, A.B., S.T.B., J.C.D., The Reception of Converts, XIV-326 pp., 1944.

199. Kowalski, Rev. Romuald Eugene, O.F.M., A.B., J.C.D., Sustenance of Religious Houses of Regulars, X-174 pp., 1944.

200. McCoy, Rev. Alan Edward, O.F.M., J.C.D., Force and Fear in Relation to Delictual Imputability and Penal Responsibility, XII-160 pp., 1944.

201. McDevitt, Rev. Vincent John, Ph.B., S.T.L., J.C.L., Perjury.

202. Martin, Rev. Thomas Owen, Ph.D., S.T.D., J.C.D., Adverse Posession, Prescription and Limitation of Actions: The Canonical "Praescriptio," XX-208 pp., 1944.

203. Miklosovic, Rev. Paul John, A.B., J.C.L., Attempted Marriages and Their Consequent Juridic Effects.

204. Mundy, Rev. Thomas Maurice, A.B., S.T.L., J.C.D., The Union of Parishes, X-164 pp., 1944.

205. O'Dea, Rev. John Coyle, A.B., J.C.D., The Matrimonial Impediment of Nonage, VIII-126 pp., 1944.

206. Olalia, Rev. Alexander Ayson, S.T.L., J.C.D., A Comparative Study of the Christian Constitution of States and the Constitution of the Philippine Commonwealth, XII-136 pp., 1944.

207. Poisson, Rev. Pierre-Marie, C.S.C., A.B., Ph.L., Th.L., J.C.L., Droits Patrimoniaux des Maisons et des Églises Religieuses.

208. Stadalnikas, Rev. Casimir Joseph, M.I.C., J.C.D., Reservation of Censures, X-141 pp., 1944.

209. Sullivan, Rev. Eugene Henry, S.T.L., J.C.D., Proof of the Reception of the Sacraments, X-165 pp., 1944.

210. Vaughan, Rev. William Edward, J.C.D., Constitutions for Diocesan Courts, X-210 pp., 1944.

211. Paro, Rev. Gino, S.T.D., J.C.D., The Right of Papal Legation, X—221 pp., 1944 (Printed 1947).

212. Balzer, Rev. Ralph Francis, C.P., J.C.D., The Computation of Time in a Canonical Novitiate, X-227 pp., 1945.

213. Dougherty, Rev. John Whelan, A.B., S.T.L., J.C.D., De Inquisitione Speciali, XII-195 pp., 1945.

214. Dziob, Rev. Michael Walter, J.C.D., The Sacred Congregation for the Oriental Church, XII-181 pp., 1945.

215. Eidenschink, Rev. John Albert, O.S.B., B.A., J.C.D., The Election of Bishops in the Letters of Pope Gregory the Great, VIII-200 pp., 1945.

216. Gill, Rev. Nicholas, C.P., J.C.D., The Spiritual Prefect in Clerical Religious Houses of Study, X-140 pp., 1945.

217. Hynes, Rev. Harry Gerard, S.T.L., J.C.D., The Privileges of Cardinals, XII-183 pp., 1945.

218. McDevitt, Rev. Gerald Vincent, S.T.L., J.C.D., The Renunciation of an Ecclesiastical Office, XIV-179 pp., 1945.

219. Manning, Rev. Joseph Leroy, J.C.D., The Free Conferral of Offices, VII-116 pp., 1945.

220. Meyer, Rev. Louis G., O.S.B., A.B., S.T.B., J.C.D., Alms-gathering by Religious, XII-163 pp., 1945.

221. O'Donnell, Rev. Cletus Francis, M.A., J.C.D., The Marriage of Minors, XII-268 pp., 1945.

222. Prunskis, Rev. Joseph, J.C.D., Comparative Law, Ecclesiastical and Civil, in Lithuanian Concordat, X-161 pp., 1945.

223. Sweeney, Rev. Francis Patrick, C.SS.R., J.C.D., The Reduction of Clerics to the Lay State, X-199 pp., 1945.

224. Vogelpohl, Rev. Henry John, J.C.D., The Simple Impediments to Holy Orders, XVI-190 pp., 1945.

225. Brockhaus, Rev. Thomas Aquinas, O.S.B., J.C.D., Religious who are known as *Conversi*, X-127 pp., 1945.

226. Griese, Rev. Orville Nicholas, S.T.D., J.C.D., The Marriage Contract and the Procreation of Offspring, XVI-224 pp., 1946.

227. Boudreaux, Rev. Warren Louis, J.C.D., The *"ab acatholicis nati"* of Canon 1099, § 2, XII-110 pp., 1946.

228. Bowe, Rev. Thomas Joseph, A.B., J.C.D., Religious Superioresses, VIII-206 pp., 1946.

229. Diederichs, Rev. Michael Ferdinand, S.C.J., J.C.D., The Jurisdiction of the Latin Ordinaries over their Oriental Subjects, XIV-153 pp., 1946.

230. Dingman, Rev. Maurice John, A.B., S.T.L., J.C.L., The Plaintiff in Contentious Trials.

231. Frison, Rev. Basil, C.M.F., M.Mus., J.C.D., The Retroactivity of Law, X-221 pp., 1946.

232. Galvin, Rev. William Anthony, M.A., J.C.D., The Administrative Transfer of Pastors, XII-288 pp., 1946.

233. GORACY, REV. JOSEPH C., J.C.L., The Diriment Matrimonial Impediment of Major Orders.

234. HALE, REV. JOSEPH FRANCIS, M.A., S.T.L., J.C.D., The Pastor of Burial, X—247 pp., 1946 (Printed 1949).

235. HENRY, REV. JOSEPH ARTHUR, A.B., J.C.D., The Mass and Holy Communion: Interritual Law, XII-138 pp., 1946.

236. LINENBERGER, REV. HERBERT, C.PP.S., J.C.D., The False Denunciation of an Innocent Confessor, VIII-205 pp., 1946 (Printed 1949).

237. LOWRY, REV. JAMES MARTIN, A.B., J.C.D., Dispensation from Private Vows, XII-266 pp., 1946.

238. LYNCH, REV. GEORGE EDWARD, A.B., S.T.L., J.C.D., Coadjutors and Auxiliaries of Bishops, X-107 pp., 1947.

239. LYNCH, REV. TIMOTHY, M.S.SS.T., J.C.D., Contracts between Bishops and Religious Congregations, XIII-232 pp., 1946.

240. MCCLUNN, REV. JUSTIN DAVID, A.B., S.T.L., J.C.D., Administrative Recourse, VII-142 pp., 1946.

241. LOHMULLER, REV. MARTIN NICHOLAS, A.B., J.C.D., The Promulgation of Law, XII-140 pp., 1947.

242. MCGRATH, REV. JAMES, A.B., J.C.D., The Privilege of the Canon, XII-156 pp., 1946.

243. MARBACH, REV. JOSEPH FRANCIS, A.B., J.C.D., Marriage Legislation for the Catholics of the Oriental Rites in the United States and Canada, XIV-314 pp., 1946.

244. SHIMKUS, REV. BERNARD ALOYSIUS, A.B., J.C.L., The Determination and Transfer of Rite.

245. SMITH, REV. VINCENT MICHAEL, A.B., S.T.L., J.C.L., Ignorance Affecting Matrimonial Consent.

246. WACHTRLE, REV. PAUL ANTHONY, A.B., J.C.L., The Baptism of the Children of Non-Catholics.

247. CROTTY, REV. MATTHEW M., J.C.D., The Recipient of First Holy Communion, X-142 pp., 1947.

248. EAGLETON, REV. GEORGE. J.C.L., The Quinquennial Faculties, Formula IV, XIV—199 pp., 1947 (Printed 1948).

249. GIBBONS, REV. MARION L., C.M., LL.B., J.C.D., Domicile of the Wife Unlawfully Separated from Her Husband, XIV-171 pp., 1947.

250. KELLY, REV. BERNARD M., S.T.L., J.C.D., The Functions Reserved to Pastors, XII-141 pp., 1947.

251. KILCULLEN, REV. THOMAS J., LL.M., J.C.D., The Collegiate Moral Person as Party Litigant, X-150 pp., 1947.

252. LAFONTAINE, REV. GERMAIN J., W.F., J.C.D., Relations Canoniques entre Le Missionnaire et Ses Superieurs, X-117 pp., 1947.

253. LANE, REV. LORAS THOMAS, B. For. Comm., A.B., S.T.L., J.C.D., Matrimonial Procedure in the Ordinary Courts of Second Instance, XVI-184 pp., 1947.

254. LOVER, REV. JAMES F., C.SS.R., M.A., J.C.D., The Master of Novices, X-168 pp., 1947.

255. MCNICHOLAS, REV. TIMOTHY JOSEPH, J.C.L., The *Septimae Manus* Witness.

256. MAROSITZ, REV. JOSEPH J., M.S.C., J.C.D., Obligations and Privileges of Religious Promoted to the Episcopal or Cardinalitial Dignities, XII-180 pp., 1947.

257. MURPHY, REV. FRANCIS J., A.B., J.C.D., Legislative Powers of the Provincial Council, XII-158 pp., 1947.

258. O'BRIEN, REV. ROMAEUS W., O. Carm., J.C.D., The Provincial Superior in Religious Orders of Men, X-294 pp., 1947.

259. PFALLER, REV. BENEDICT A., O.S.B., J.C.D., The *Ipso Facto* Effected Dismissal of Religious, XII-225 pp., 1947.

260. POPEK, REV. ALPHONSE S., M.A., J.C.D., The Rights and Obligations of Metropolitans, XX-460 pp., 1947.

261. RISTUCCIA, REV. BERNARD JOSEPH, C.M., J.C.D., Quasi-Religious, XVI—318 pp., 1947 (Printed 1949).

262. SONNTAG, REV. NATHANIEL L., O.F.M., Cap., J.C.D., Censorship of Special Classes of Books, XII-147 pp., 1947.

263. STADLER, REV. JOSEPH NICHOLAS, J.C.D., Frequent Holy Communion, X-158 pp., 1947.

264. SZAL, REV. IGNATIUS JOSEPH, J.C.D., The Communication of Catholics with Schismatics, XII-217 pp., 1947.

265. WAGNER, REV. URBAN S., O.F.M. Conv., J.C.D., Parochial Substitute Vicars and Supplying Priests, IX-126 pp., 1947.

266. QUINN, REV. JOSEPH, M.A., J.C.D., Documents Required for the Reception of Orders, XII-207 pp., 1948.

267. BENNINGTON, REV. JAMES CLEMENT, A.B., J.C.L., The Recipient of Confirmation.

268. BLAHER, REV. DAMIAN JOSEPH, O.F.M., A.B., J.C.L., The Ordinary Processes in Causes of Beatification and Canonization.

269. CLUNE, REV. ROBERT BELL, B.A., J.C.L., The Judicial Interrogation of the Parties.

270. COURTEMANCHE, REV. BASIL F., B.A., J.C.L., The Total Simulation of Matrimonial Consent.

271. DLOUHY, REV. MAUR JOHN, O.S.B., A.B., J.C.L., The Ordination of Exempt Religious.

272. DONOVAN, REV. JOHN THOMAS, PH.B., S.T.L., J.C.D., The Clerical Obligations of Canons 138 and 140, XII—209 pp., 1948.

273. FREKING, REV. FREDERICK W., A.B., S.T.B., J.C.L., The Canonical Installation of Pastors.

274. FULTON, REV. THOMAS B., J.C.L., Prenuptial Investigation.

275. GODLEY, REV. JAMES P., J.C.L., The Time and the Place for the Celebration of Mass.

276. KANE, REV. THOMAS A., A.B., B.S., J.C.L., Jurisdiction of Patriarchs until 1439.

277. KENNEDY, REV. ANDREW A., J.C.L., The Annual Pastoral Report to the Local Ordinary.

278. KONRAD, REV. JOSEPH GEORGE, J.C.L., Transfer of Religious.

279. KRESS, REV. ALPHONSE, J.C.L., Contumacy in Ecclesiastical Trials.

280. MCCARTNEY, REV. MARCELLUS ANTHONY, O.F.M., M.A., J.C.L., Faculties of Regular Confessors.

281. MCCASLIN, REV. EDWARD PATRICK, M.A., S.T.L., J.C.L., The Division of Parishes.

282. MCELROY, REV. FRANCIS J., A.B., J.C.L., The Privileges of Bishops.

283. QUINN, REV. STEPHEN, M. S. SS. T., J.C.D., Relation between the Local Ordinary and Religious of Diocesan Approval, XII—153 pp., 1948 (Printed 1949).

284. SCHNEIDER, REV. EDELHARD LOUIS, A.D.S., M.A., J.C.D., The Status of Secularized Ex-Religious Clerics, X-155 pp., 1948.

285. THOMPSON, REV. CHESTER J., A.B., J.C.L., The Simple Removal from Office.

286. O'BRIEN, REV. KENNETH R., A.B., J.C.D., The Nature of Support of Diocesan Priests in the United States, XVI-162 pp., 1949.

287. METZ, REV. JOHN E., S.T.L., J.C.D., The Recording Judge in the Ecclesiastical Collegiate Tribunal, X-130 pp., 1949.

288. REINHARDT, REV. MARION J., J.C.L., The Rogatory Commission.

289. ORTEGA UHINK, REV. JUAN, S.J., J.C.L., De Delicto Sollicitationis.

290. CASEY, REV. JAMES V., J.C.L., A Study of Canon 2222, § 1.

291. ALLGEIER, REV. JOSEPH L., J.C.L., The Canonical Obligation of Preaching in Parochial Churches.

292. CAHILL, REV. DANIEL R., J.C.L., The Custody of the Holy Eucharist.

293. CARR, REV. AIDAN, O.F.M. CONV., S.T.D., J.C.L., Vocation to the Priesthood: Its Canonical Concept.

294. KNOPKE, REV. ROCH, F., O.F.M., J.C.L., Reverential Fear in Matrimonial Cases in Asiatic Countries.

295. Lavelle, Rev. Howard D., J.C.L., The Obligation of Holding Sacred Missions in Parishes.

296. Michells, Rev. Anthony B., J.C.L., The Constitutive Elements of Parishes.

297. Noone, Rev. John J., J.C.L., Nullity in Judicial Acts.

298. Sheehan, Rev. Daniel E., J.C.L., The Minister of Holy Communion.

299. Statkus, Rev. Francis J., J.C.L., The Minister of the Last Sacraments.

300. Cook, Rev. John P., J.C.L., Ecclesiastical Communities and Their Ability to Induce Legal Customs.

301. Fazzalaro, Rev. Francis J., J.C.L., The Place for the Hearing of Confessions.

302. Hannan, Philip M., J.C.L., The Canonical Concept of *congrua sustentatio* for the Secular Clergy.

www.ingramcontent.com/pod-product-compliance
Lightning Source LLC
LaVergne TN
LVHW050208080826
844660LV00012B/380

* 9 7 8 0 8 1 3 2 2 4 6 6 4 *